real-life
wisdom
from a
**mother
of ten**

Kathryn Sansone

Woman First
family always

Meredith® Books
Des Moines, Iowa

Meredith Books
1716 Locust Street
Des Moines, Iowa 50309-3023
www.meredithbooks.com

First Edition. Printed in the United States of America.
Library of Congress Control Number: 2005931899
ISBN: 0-696-22832-7

I dedicate this book in thanksgiving to God and our Blessed Mother for guiding me in my life's journey as a woman, wife, and mother; to my beautiful husband Jim who has been my best friend and constant support and love of my life since the moment I met him when I was 16 years old; and to our most precious children and greatest blessing in our lives, Jimmy, Big, Nikko, Lan, Stefan, Sophia, Anthony, Carmen, Marianna, and Marco. They brighten our days and fill our hearts with pride and joy. I could not have written this book without them.

Contents

Introduction

You've probably picked up this book because you're looking for advice. Maybe you had a rough morning with the kids—before you even downed your morning coffee, you were screaming at someone. Or that ever-growing pile of laundry and your work schedule are dueling it out, and the laundry is losing the battle. Or your spouse seems frustrated with you, but he's not fessing up. Or perhaps you're simply drowning in responsibilities and worries, and you're wondering how on earth you can do it all. Not to mention that you'd like to do it all well. After all, it's your family we're talking about: your children, your husband, your home. I know just how you feel. Welcome to the club.

The fact that I have ten children between the ages of eight months and eighteen, live in a well-organized home, have a happy and fulfilling marriage, and am content with how I look should not make me special. But it has—not so much in my eyes, but in the eyes of thousands of people who read my story in *O, The Oprah Magazine* or saw me on her show.

A Turning Point

It all began when three of my girlfriends and I went to Chicago for my fortieth birthday to see *The Oprah Winfrey Show*. I had been a longtime fan, and for me, attending the taping of a show was the perfect way to celebrate. After the show, Oprah began asking the audience how they stay fit (one of her favorite topics). I raised my hand and told her that weight training has been the easiest, fastest way I have found to stay in shape—and I was still doing it even though I was six months pregnant at the time. When Oprah asked me how many kids I have, I answered, "Eight with one on the way." That's when Oprah brought me up on stage and asked me more questions about how I looked so fit after having eight children. I gladly shared with her my physical routine.

A few weeks later on a Saturday afternoon, I was in my kitchen enjoying some peace and quiet while the kids were outside playing when the phone rang. A cheerful voice said, "Kathryn? This is *The Oprah Winfrey Show* calling."

"Oh, stop," I said laughing, believing that one of my children was playing a practical joke on me—since I had been to Chicago, I was more impressed by Oprah than ever.

But this wasn't a joke.

First Contact

One of Oprah's producers then invited me to be a guest on an upcoming show devoted to how different women stay in shape through weight training. A few weeks later Oprah was introducing me as "poster woman for fitness," featuring me as a busy mom who stays fit through weight training. After that, Oprah's magazine editor contacted me, asking if I were interested in doing the *Oprah* interview for the May Mother's Day issue of the magazine. Of course I was interested!

Just a few days later, Oprah arrived at my home. The moment she stepped out of her car, she entered my life—

literally. She scooped up my 3-year-old daughter and very quickly blended into the usual mayhem at the Sansone house. After having some lunch, we all headed downstairs to the basement to show Oprah our sports court, a gymnasium-style space outfitted with a basketball net, a hockey goal, and other indoor sports equipment. Oprah joined in on the boys' basketball game until she was out of breath, and then the kids put on some music and everyone—Oprah included—started dancing. We were all stunned: How could Oprah, a superstar, be so normal? Her authenticity and love of life were so apparent, I became an even bigger fan.

Oprah spent most of the day with us, wanting to really get to know my family. She observed how I organize my home from top to bottom, how I feed my small army of children, and how I get through the day with a smile on my face when my husband comes home from work (although that day was Sunday and Jim was home). She also invited me to sit down with her for a quiet, more intimate chat to get to know me better. After discussing the practical aspects of my life, Oprah wanted to find out what made me tick on the inside. She referred to me as the role model of motherhood—quite a hefty title, but one that makes me think I may be able to affect a wider group of women with some practical advice that has helped me through the years. Indeed it was the gist of that conversation almost two years ago that inspired me to write this book.

And now with yet another baby in my arms, I am ready to share it all with you.

Since my "Oprah moment," I began to reflect on what makes my life work smoothly and happily—not only in spite of my having ten children, two dogs, a husband, and a house to maintain but also because of these facts. I realized that there are three essential truths that keep me sane when life gets crazy, content when life is running smoothly, and afloat when life threatens to drown my spirit.

Far from Perfect

The first is that I'm not supermom. I know I'm not perfect—far from it—and, actually, I don't try to be. One of the most important lessons I've learned over the past eighteen years is that not only is it impossible to be supermom, I don't want to be. Like any mother, I get tired, I get crabby, I get angry. Some days I seem to have the patience of a saint. Other days I totally lose it and scream at my kids. And sometimes I just go on strike. But to me, this is the normal cycle of any family. We may argue, struggle, and fight, but at the end of the day, we can all look at one another and get in touch with that place deep inside where love dwells. I am happy, Jim is happy, and my kids are happy. We are a team, we're on a journey through life, and we're doing pretty well.

Taking Care of Me

The second is that I am important—as a woman and an individual, not simply as a mother and wife. I've learned that if a woman gives up one aspect of herself—the woman in her, the mother, or the wife—the other two facets suffer. Often women think the opposite: that if they just concentrate on being good mothers (preferably, perfect mothers), then they'll automatically be good women and wives. Nothing could be further from the truth.

A woman must be aware of herself and her own needs so she can be aware of the needs of her family. If you give too much of yourself away in the process of being a parent, you'll probably end up feeling stressed and resentful. Resenting your family will poison your honest efforts. You may not even know why you're feeling this way and apply yourself even more diligently to selfless activities to make up for it. Soon everyone will be unhappy, simply because you haven't given yourself the respect or attention that you deserve. Women don't need to feel guilty about taking care of themselves, because it will only help them do a better job of caring for others. You must take care of yourself first for everyone else's sake, as well as for your own.

A Spiritual Core

The third essential truth is that a content woman, one who is at ease with herself regardless of how busy her life is, must stay connected to her spiritual core. Whether it comes from religion, family, exercise, or somewhere else doesn't matter— every woman needs a place to retreat to when her soul cries out for nourishment. I think of the spiritual core as that unspoken place in a woman's heart where her spirit lives. It's the place where I talk to God; it's the place a person goes to when she wants to hear the truth. It's a peaceful, comforting, endlessly giving place, and we can all find it—it sometimes just gets buried in clutter!

I am privileged to have grown up with a strong sense of God, which helps me deal with my daily struggles. But if you feel this is a void in your life, don't despair! This book will share with you ways to find that core of serenity, from reaching out to other parents to reconnecting with your extended family to pursuing an old hobby or letting yourself sink into the psychological peace of yoga practice. You owe it to yourself to focus on finding the way to your own heart.

These three core wisdoms—that I am not supermom, that I am important as a woman first and then as a wife and mother, and that I must make time to nourish my spiritual center—underlie the many stories and tips in this book. I believe that every woman, regardless of how many roles she juggles, not only has the power to be in control of her life but has the innate ability to pull it all off with great aplomb and joy.

Lessons Learned

Often when people first meet me—at social gatherings or my children's school or in the grocery store—they ask me for advice on how I manage my ever-growing brood and still remain so sane and fit. "You make everything look so easy," they say. "Do you have a secret?" When I respond, "There's no secret," most people don't believe it. They look at their own lives in progress and think I must take a magic pill every morning.

I don't. The techniques I use are not secret, and the way I choose to approach my life and my relationships is not especially fancy or complicated. They are the results of the lessons I've learned over the years that help me stay in control and also feel real fulfillment. Eighteen years ago, when I gave birth to my first child, I didn't know how to handle every situation I faced. A trip to the grocery store seemed to take half a day. If I happened to see another mother with four or five kids in tow, I wondered, "How can she even manage shopping?" I then returned home feeling dejected, overwhelmed, and determined to get as much done as possible while the baby was napping. At breakneck speed, I would try to clean the house, mow the lawn(!), and make dinner. It was no surprise that by evening I was exhausted and irritable. I had no energy for my child and certainly nothing left to give my husband. Something had to give.

Slowly but surely, as child after child was born, I began to get the hang of it. I realized that I could accomplish so much more than a trip to the grocery store if I put some priorities in place. But the first thing I learned to do was to take time for myself each and every day. I knew that I would have so much more to give if I first filled my own cup. So I began to set aside time just for me: to work out, to connect with a friend, to get a manicure, or to plan a date with my husband. What I did did not seem to matter as much as the fact that I did something for me that made me feel replenished, refreshed, and recharged. I not only became much better able to get everything done, I felt much more fulfilled doing so.

The Bottom Line

But the bottom line is this: I'm where I am today, with a happy and successful family alongside me on this journey, because I try to take it all one small step at a time. I keep my expectations in check and remember to take care of myself so I can take care of my children and my husband.

This book is the result of years of thinking and doing and being a wife and mother of ten kids, as well as the wisdom gained from my most important role models—my parents, and, since meeting Jim, his parents. It's also the outcome of figuring out—through trial and error—what is the best balance among my self, my family, and my relationship. For it has become clear to me that for most mothers, life falls into three major categories: Your Self, Your Marriage, and Your Family and Kids. This book explores those areas and the many questions that crop up within them. For instance: Who are you, and if you don't know anymore, how can you find yourself again? Are you able to say no? Did you know that small indulgences ward off the blues and big ones get you in trouble? In "Your Marriage," I explore how to keep your marriage strong and joyful. There may be bumps on the road, but there are also some great detours and beautiful sights and a lot of fun to be had along the way!

Did you know there's a productive way to argue? And that a little lipstick goes a long way? In the "Your Family & Kids" section, I look at some tricks of the trade that have helped me manage what to most people seems like an impossible task: running a household with so many kids! I talk about writing love letters to my children and figuring out how to relate to teachers. I question some of the accepted norms and offer suggestions for learning to trust your instincts. This format will allow you to dip in and out of the book, learning from my personal experiences and drawing helpful conclusions about your own life as you read.

This is a book of what I call "real-life wisdom"—practical tips and insights that help me get through the day. Sometimes when I feel exhausted, I focus on some simple words of wisdom that help fortify my spirit. Others are practical ideas that make me more efficient at getting the laundry done, dinner on the table, and my kids bathed before bed (almost every night!). And still others are personal, quirky pieces of advice: How do you stay interested in your mate when life feels like a roller coaster? How do you maintain the connection to each other as partners when you're exhausted? For me, I make a conscious effort to give my husband TLC (aka Tender Loving Care). I make sure I tell him how important he is to the kids, what they say about him, and how much they love him. I know that, after a long day at work, he will soon forget his miseries and remember why he loves me.

Incorporated in this small book of wisdom are also the experiences, thoughts, and feelings of other women with whom I have spoken and who have influenced me. We're all in this together, doing the best we can. I hope that a few helpful hints from other women in the same boat will offer you a moment's peace on a hectic day and the vision of a life beyond its current state of chaos.

If I can do it, you can too!

Perspective

Sometimes life does not go quite as planned. You have the best intentions, but something throws you for a loop. Or you're doing everything you've been told, and it's still not working. For instance, I recently dumped time-outs. They may work for some kids, but mine seemed to enjoy this time spent in their rooms. I wondered what lesson was being learned. So I came up with a more effective strategy: Chores! Not only do the children learn that there are consequences to bad behavior, but I get my trash taken out, the dishwasher unloaded, or the room picked up. Even a 3-year-old can handle a simple chore such as sweeping.

For those moments when you need to laugh and get your sense of perspective back, I've included sidebars that either point out the funny side of disaster or get right to the nitty-gritty about what to do when things go wrong. Topics include the top six hilarious things that my children have said or done, how to support your children when you can't physically be there for them, and eight ways to instantly relax when you just need a break.

I enjoy being with my kids, so I'm a hands-on parent. But I also ask for help when I need it—which is often. I ask for help from my husband, a babysitter, friend, or family member. I don't feel guilty or resentful, because I know I am giving it my best shot. That's really the most anyone can do.

This book aims to give all women—single mothers, working women, mothers with one child or twelve, with lots of money or just enough—the inspiration and know-how to manage life with less stress so they, too, can begin and end each day feeling fulfilled, with their sense of humor and sense of self still intact. It sounds like a tall order, but take it from me, it's not. We're all on a long journey and we're learning as we go along. If nothing else this book will show you that you're not flying solo. By reading this advice you'll have started the process of reaching out and giving yourself the support that you need and deserve.

Your Self

How to use this book

In this section, you will find 30 brief reflections—each a mix of helpful tips often illustrated with anecdotes from my own experiences as a woman, wife, and mother—that will teach you to rediscover the power of your own spirit. Take it one day at a time. Instead of viewing my tips as more pressure—yet another to-do list—use them as reminders to slow down and think about you for a change. Then go at your own pace: Read a tip each day or whenever you want some fresh ideas and inspiration.

Your Self

As women, wives, and mothers, most of us have heard or uttered the very tired phrase "a mother's work is never done" many times. We can all share stories of how difficult, stressful, and exhausting it is to try to do everything—take care of our kids, run our households, work, and maintain a meaningful relationship—preferably all at the same time. And it's true: managing all these aspects of our lives is difficult, stressful, and exhausting. But does it have to be?

When I was younger and only had two children, life seemed much harder. I spent my days going from one task to another without so much as taking a breath, never mind a bath. The word *drudgery* comes to mind. At the end of the day, yes, the beds were made, the house tidy, the dinner cooked. But it seemed the moments of joy came only infrequently and the negative feelings powered by fatigue and time spent doing everything for others were much more frequent.

Baby Steps

Then, slowly but surely, and through a lot of trial and error, I began to understand that unless I took care of myself, everything in life would seem too difficult, too unmanageable, and definitely not enjoyable. It came down to a choice I alone could make: Was I ready to take care of myself, or would I let myself get pulled down the road where a negative, powerless attitude toward life holds sway? I chose the former, and it has made all the difference.

Of course, this new way of living my life didn't happen overnight. I started by taking baby steps. I decided that each day I would do one small thing for myself—whether it was spending twenty minutes on the treadmill with my younger son balanced on the top, putting together some cash to pay a babysitter for a short-but-luxurious hour so I could get my nails done, or simply figuring out a way to take a ten-minute shower instead just squeezing in a two-minute one. Though small, the impact of these baby steps was immediate and dramatic: I felt remarkably better in my own skin. I felt stronger—physically and emotionally. I felt better able to tackle the rest of the day, juggling trips to the grocery store, doing errands, and taking care of my growing brood.

The Domino Effect

That's the lesson that I'd like to share with other exhausted, overwhelmed moms out there. When you neglect any one of these aspects of yourself, it has a negative domino effect in which you lose your center and feel disconnected from yourself and others. On the other hand when you stay connected to yourself and learn ways to nurture yourself, managing everything else in your life becomes easier.

I connect to myself in three ways: emotionally, physically, and spiritually.

My inner self. When I stay in touch with my inner self, my former self, and my friends, I stay grounded and better able to manage my daily life, which is filled to the brim with action.

My body. When I take care of my body, strengthening and

making it feel fit and vital, I feel better about myself—on the inside and the outside. When I feel better about myself, my confidence soars and I feel hopeful, capable, and ready to handle even the biggest challenges.

My spirit. When I am spiritually centered, I feel both close to my soul and to God. I feel more connected to the world all around me, and it's this dual connection—at both the level of the soul and to the larger world—that ultimately gives my life the most meaning.

I learned to take care of myself gradually, and I continue to learn valuable lessons about how best to do that. Now—ten children and nineteen years of marriage later—I can say that on most evenings, when my husband walks through the door I can smile. Easier said than done? Maybe. As with anything important, taking care of yourself requires both conscious commitment and action.

First, you need to develop an attitude toward life that matches your behavior so that when you intend for something to happen, it actually does happen.

Second, taking care of yourself also means staying focused on your priorities while at the same time giving yourself a break when you need to.

"And while I never forget that I am my children's mother and my husband's wife, I know that I must always remain connected to me, to who I am as a woman."

1. Who Are You?

Who me? Yes, you. This may at first appear to be a simple question, but it's not. As our lives become more multifaceted, so do our identities. We are no longer simply someone's daughter, sister, or friend. We are women with a host of roles to fulfill. A modern mother's job title might read: disciplinarian, healer, event planner, soothsayer, cook, chauffeur, tutor, psychologist, coach, career woman, cleaner, social coordinator, school liaison representative . . . The list can go on . . . and on . . . and on! This multitasking was recently underscored when AOL asked me to join a group of women they call CEOs—Chief Everything Officers. AOL was organizing a forum to discuss the fact that modern-day women—especially mothers—are more accurately described as "family managers" because they juggle so many roles when they raise kids, run households, and manage the day-to-day lives of their children and family.

It's no wonder many women feel like they are drowning under the pressure to juggle all these various tasks. How do we keep our heads above water? How can we do a good job and feel satisfied with our roles as CEOs? Many women are voicing such questions, not just to me, but in magazines, to their friends, and to their therapists. How can we do it all????

Remaining Connected
Sometimes modern mothers are asked to operate outside of their comfort zones, taking on new and daunting duties daily.

In juggling all of these responsibilities, we often get stuck defining ourselves by just one role, that of mother. And while I never forget that I am my children's mother and my husband's wife, I know that I must always remain connected to me, to who I am as a woman.

This wasn't always easy for me to do, regardless of how much I have accomplished. When I was first married and had three children in four years, I just went through my days, trying to get as much done as possible. Jim worked long hours, there was much less money, and I was alone for long stretches of time with three kids in diapers. I was younger, but I was definitely in lesser shape—in both my body and my mind. By the end of the day, all I could manage was to crawl into bed. I spent many hours fretting, complaining, and envying Jim and everyone else. Then it dawned on me: I was being a martyr, feeling sorry for myself, as if I had no power over my own life. Time to take action!

Action Plan!

In a short time, I had figured out how to salvage 30-minute breaks once or twice a day to work out. This is when Jim first introduced me to weightlifting. As I began to integrate a workout into my (almost) daily routine, I felt immediately better—I was calmer, I had more energy, and my mood was remarkably more positive! I had made a simple change, but one that had a huge impact on my daily life. Learning to take care of myself in a physical way opened the door to the idea that I am in the driver's seat of my own life—whether I have one, four, or ten kids.

All of us are trying to be the best mothers possible. But we often forget that before we can be good, confident mothers, we have to take care of ourselves and learn how to make time for ourselves when we need it. For me, this means that I do something for myself in three ways: I make sure I stay physically, emotionally, and spiritually fit. I work out at least four times each week. I take the time and effort to keep up with friends, no matter how busy I am; and I find time each day—even if it's just ten minutes—to connect with my soul.

So ask yourself:

- Are you taking care of your body by exercising at least two or three times each week?
- Are you making sure your heart is healthy by staying connected to those people in your life whom you love and who love you?
- Are you paying attention to your spirit by nourishing it with enough quiet time to hear yourself think?

Allow Yourself to Dream

Periodically we need to think back to who we were before marriage and motherhood so we can find ways to reenergize those dreams and skills and further develop them. Do you dream of picking up a paintbrush again? Hacking away at that novel you've always wanted to write? Training for an athletic goal? Do you fantasize about picking up knitting or sewing again? Listening to your heart and acting on its desires is about exploring a goal, not necessarily conquering it. There's no need to fear failure, because the goal is to explore, not conquer.

When I first thought of writing this book, I thought, "No way." I wasn't a writer. I had no prior experience with writing more than a term paper in college. How was I going to write a book of advice for other women? But I believed so fully in my desire to share what I've done and learned over the years that I pursued the project with vigor, finding support, help, and courage along the way.

In striving to succeed as best we can in our roles as caretakers of our precious families, we must work hard at validating and exploring our own needs and desires. Ultimately this commitment to ourselves will make us better women, wives, and mothers. Allow yourself to dream, encourage yourself to try something new, and do it!

2. Keep Your Personal History Alive

We are not exactly who we were ten, fifteen, twenty years ago. Through our experiences, our joys, our sorrows, our successes, and our failures, we constantly change with each passing year. Everything we experience in our lives impacts us in some way, profound or subtle. And each of our roles has made us who we are today. Indeed we are a unique combination of events and experiences. When we look back at these parts of ourselves, we give ourselves the opportunity to see how we've changed and grown. Looking back also reminds us of perhaps forgotten attributes or talents upon which we can draw today. I recently came across a picture of myself at thirteen that ran in the local newspaper. Gangly and awkward with my baseball cap on backwards, there I was smiling from ear to ear, telling the local reporter about the camp I was running in my backyard for neighborhood kids. I had transformed my garage into various stations: arts and crafts, story hour, a water table, and other activities. At thirteen I didn't have time to get nervous or overthink whether or not I could run the camp—I just did it! And what do you know? It was a great success. Why? Because my small campers had a great time.

Ideals in Action

When I was nineteen, I decided to walk on to a college volleyball team. By volleyball standards, the odds were

Simple Words of Wisdom

Taking care of one's self does not happen automatically. You have to make a conscious decision to do so. But you can begin by taking these baby steps each day. When you start by putting aside a minute or two, you give yourself the chance to make that minute grow into an hour.

- **Reaffirm who you are** each morning you wake up by acknowledging your strengths.

- **Create quiet time** each day to be alone and connect with your spirit—to pray, to listen to yourself, or simply to be in God's presence.

- **Do something positive** for someone else at least once a day—without seeking anything in return.

- **Move.** Putting your body in motion will lift your spirits, strengthen your body, and ease your stress.

- **Ease your mind** by decluttering one space in your house each day—even if it's just one drawer of your dresser.

- **Choose to look on the bright side.** Making a conscious decision to face the world in an optimistic way will boost your self-confidence and empower you—and optimism is contagious!

- **Be grateful** for your children, your spouse, your self. Be grateful that you are alive.

against me: I was not that tall, I was fairly thin, and the team was already a tight group of girls, not exactly welcoming to a newcomer. But I committed to it. I worked out twice a day for two four-hour sessions, one in the morning and another in the afternoon. I would come home bruised and exhausted. And because of the long workouts, no matter how much I ate, I began to lose weight—I went from thin to downright scrawny. My friends kept telling me to quit, that it was just too hard. But there was no way I was going to quit. In the end, I not only became a member of the team, but I even made captain.

Now whenever I start to feel depleted and overwhelmed by all that I have to do, I think back to myself at thirteen, when I had the energy and spunk to run a camp, and at nineteen, when I persevered and didn't give up my goal of joining a college volleyball team. I get in touch with that part of myself that believes in herself, acts on ideas, and doesn't worry about the outcome. To this day, these memories remind me of how much I'm capable of doing.

Finding Perspective

We all have memories of ourselves and things we are proud of, and it's important that we recall these instances to remind ourselves of all we have accomplished and been through.

How do we keep our history alive? By staying in touch with our past, keeping or reading a diary, calling an old friend from high school or college, going to a reunion, or looking through photo albums and scrapbooks. Remembering where we've been helps us keep life in perspective and urges us not to take life so seriously all the time. Sure there are times when we all have to be serious, but many times, our reactions to experiences and events are out of proportion to the reality of the whole picture. By looking at your past self, you stay in touch with the real you, the person underneath who has moved with you, grown with you, cried and laughed with you. You keep *you* in perspective.

3. Establish Your Limits

Over the years I've come to realize that in order for me to manage all that I have to do, I need to stay clear on my different roles so I don't become a muddled mess, stretched too thin, and unsure of who I am. And it's this clarity that makes life run smoothly.

Do you have trouble turning down or delegating work? Are you exhausted? For your own sanity, learning to say no will liberate you from the stress of overcommitment. Your family and friends will be grateful, and you will feel like a new woman—one who is capable and in control.

I know this firsthand. I've always been the go-to person in my family. Growing up as the middle daughter, my role was that of peacemaker and diplomat. People came to me to settle arguments, ask my advice, and help sort out confusing issues. And while I am happy to be there for my family and friends, there comes a time when I have to simply say no. I can be stretched too thin, with not enough of me to go around. I remember one spring, when I learned an important lesson about saying no and slowing down.

Notice Signals

At the time I was coaching for two kids' sports teams, pregnant with my eighth child, and, of course, managing the lives and home of the rest of the family. And while I am pretty agile at juggling a lot of balls in the air, I started to notice signs that all was not well: I was being short and impatient with my kids, a bit naggy with Jim, and I was always tired—no matter how much or little sleep I got the night before. When I went to see my OB/GYN for a regular prenatal checkup, he told me that I had placenta previa and immediately put me on bed rest. My doctor was confident that the baby and I would be fine, but he was concerned about what was going on in my life outside the pregnancy. I described my daily routine, my sleep habits, and how I was feeling. For me, being put on bed rest was a wake-up call: I had to slow down. This warning from my doctor stopped me short: I knew I was doing too much, and I just had to stop. I quickly reassessed my commitments and downsized, reducing the number of my obligations. Thankfully, the rest of the pregnancy went smoothly and without complications. But I learned an invaluable lesson: Pay attention to your body's signals, your mind's signals, and the signals of those around you. You may need to cut some things out of your life to maintain the best balance for you—and your family.

The Art of Delegating

Feeling guilty? Decide right now to banish that feeling. Of course, many people have trouble turning things down: They feel like a failure if they can't live up to every request made of them. If you're like this, examining the root cause of this behavior will help you.

Sometimes we take on too much because we feel insecure and want people to like us. Well, people will still like us even if we can't take on every project—and if they don't, then we shouldn't worry about them. It's just not worth it. We can't be everything to everybody; we must establish priorities in order to lead a balanced life.

Or perhaps the problem is that you're too confident in your own abilities to let someone else take the reins for a change. Most likely you're not the only one who can do things right. Delegating wisely is a fine art. The most successful people in business, politics, and the home are those who know how to hand off certain tasks to others.

At the end of each summer before the new school year begins, I make an inventory of all the activities I'll be involved in. I want to make sure I haven't overextended myself and that I have left enough time in my schedule to realistically accomplish all I need to do. Sometimes things have to go. Last year I withdrew from a PTA committee. This year I decided to sign back on. Each year some new challenge presents itself.

How many school/home/work projects can you handle well, without sacrificing downtime for yourself and your family? Once you've figured this out, politely and firmly turn down all other requests for committee work or volunteering. Better to do a few things thoroughly and well than many things poorly.

Schedule Accordingly

If you know your own capabilities and have a practical mind-set, you'll be amazed at both your efficiency and the increase in satisfaction you experience. So how do you get started?

- First, decide what activities you are interested in pursuing.

- Second, determine how many activities your schedule allows. As a side note, I never spend more than five years serving on any particular board.

- Third, prioritize the activities according to their value and importance.

- Choose and commit to those activities.

- Stick to your guns!

Because I understand and accept that I cannot do everything, my life is not as frantic as you might imagine. Thank goodness!

4. Stay in Touch with How You Feel

We move so swiftly through our days, sometimes we don't even take the time to notice how we feel. And yet, our feelings are the most honest ways we communicate with ourselves. Are you hungry? Tired? Uneasy? Need to be alone? Lonely and in need of company? Are you feeling anxious? Yes, I am dwelling on negative feelings here. But for a reason: When we feel good, centered, happy, we flow through our days with ease. But when we get stuck in negative emotions, just getting through the day can feel overwhelming. Recognize those negative emotions and put them to positive use. They are simply signals that you need and deserve some TLC.

Our bodies are terrific barometers for how we are feeling. I try to listen to my body, and when something hurts, I know something is up. My back will hurt. My legs ache. I have a headache. These are all signs that I'm neglecting something that needs to be dealt with, and it's usually a feeling that is pent up. Sometimes I am not aware of how I am feeling and have to listen to people around me. Jim can look at me and see what's going on. He'll say, "Go take a break," or "Sleep in tomorrow; I'll handle it." I am so caught up in the busyness of daily life that I have stopped paying attention to how I feel. And when this happens, I begin to crash.

The next time you sense that negative feelings are getting in your way, try this simple exercise:

1. Stand still or sit down.

2. Do a quick scan of your body.

3. Recognize any strain or tension you feel.

4. Focus on that area.

5. Take a deep breath, keeping that area in mind.

6. Exhale.

7. Repeat until you feel the tension ebb or disappear.

Once your body releases the tension, it's time to identify the feeling itself. Are you sad? Disappointed? Afraid? Nervous? One good way to release negative feelings is to simply name them. Once we say to ourselves, "I'm sad today," we begin to feel some relief from the negative feeling, having simply recognized how we feel. And once we acknowledge our feelings, we are then clearheaded enough to figure out what is causing those feelings and what we can do to change the situation. Of course, some situations can't be changed. But by being more connected to your feelings and their source, we are able to choose to be positive. We tend to feel more hopeful that such feelings are more manageable or will eventually subside or pass. Indeed, the more we stay in touch with how we feel, the less our lives are impacted by such negative feelings. So next time you feel bombarded by difficult emotions, sit still and try to name that feeling. In the same way we help our kids name their feelings and teach them that feelings come and go, we need to remind ourselves that our own feelings also ebb and flow.

5. Simply Ask for Help

No one expects mothers to be superheroes, except mothers themselves! We must free ourselves from unrealistic expectations by learning to ask for help when we need it. Suffering in silence won't do anyone any good. Accepting that we cannot always be everything to everyone is wisdom well worth acquiring.

With ten kids, it is physically impossible for me to be everywhere at once. I can only drop so many kids off at games, take kids to doctor appointments, pick up others from school and practice. On weekends Jim and I usually split up and share driving responsibilities. But during the week I am on my own unless I ask for help, which I do regularly. I ask my mom, my sisters, my neighbors. I have even asked a coach if he could take my sons to games! Asking for help doesn't necessarily require money for a babysitter or day care. You can ask for (and receive) help in many ways:

- Call a friend and ask her if she has time to take your kids for an hour or so—(and, yes, offer to do the same for her some time).
- E-mail your husband at work to tell him you're feeling stretched thin. Would he be willing to come home early one night this week?
- Figure out a way to hire a babysitter so you can be free to do what you need to do.
- Ask your kids, your neighbors' kids, or a neighbor for help. I am lucky in that my older kids can now drive and help

me with the carpool, going to the store, cleaning the car, and going to the dry cleaner. But I also ask my younger kids to help with household chores, everything from sweeping the kitchen floor to vacuuming to loading and unloading the dishwasher. As your kids grow, it's important to involve them in chores and household activities. I always get my kids to help at dinnertime, giving each of them something to do—set the table, fold the napkins, fill water glasses, and clear the table.

If your kids are not yet old enough to help you or one another, perhaps there is an older kid in the neighborhood who is willing to do some chores for a small amount of money. I have a friend who is the mother of three kids under four. She barters with a twelve-year-old boy in her neighborhood: When he helps her around the house, she lets him borrow their bike twice a week.

Ask for Outside Help

Asking for help isn't easy, but it is necessary, so don't be shy. Ask a neighbor to come over to play with and occupy your 2-year-old so you can do bills, take a shower, nap, or do a quick workout. Do you have a teenage nephew or niece? Ask him or her to take the dog to the vet or to take the kids to get haircuts.

Also remember to look outside the four walls of your home to gather advice from different sources. Consider these ideas:

• A librarian can steer you to useful self-help books, especially when it comes to child-rearing issues.

- Make a date with a friend who shares your values and find out how she would approach your issue.
- Find a psychologist who can give you unbiased, expert feedback; this can take a lot of pressure off. You might get new ideas about how to tackle a problem or recognize your own ability to come up with solutions.

Many people like to feel needed. Last year when it was my turn to host the annual Christmas party for my book club, I just couldn't do it. I was at the end of my first trimester with my tenth pregnancy, and I was simply exhausted. When I

Breaking the Taboo of Seeking Professional Help

I am a firm believer in asking for professional support when problems or issues seem too big or overwhelming. It saddens me to hear that seeking the advice or support from a psychotherapist or psychiatrist still carries a stigma. I have watched several close acquaintences suffer needlessly because of their reluctance to ask for help.

So the next time you feel that a problem is bigger than you are, or if that problem has caused you to lose sleep, suffer increased anxiety, or impact your life in another way, then it may be time for you to consider seeking professional help. A therapist can offer you confidentiality, emotional safety, and objectivity—qualities that are often difficult to find among our family and friends.

admitted this to my book club friends, they said to me, "If you just open your doors, we will do everything else!" And they did; they were terrific and so was the party.

Friends and neighbors sometimes enjoy lending a helping hand: I'm not shy about asking someone to pick up a child, bring a dish to a dinner party, or occupy my kids for a few hours. They can always say no! Simply asking for advice or help from friends or neighbors is not a burden. Just remember to listen, and always return favors. But most of all, be honest with yourself about how and when you need help. If you wait until the last moment, when you are in tears on the bathroom floor or wanting to hit your head against the wall, you've waited too long! Pay attention to your signals: Are you feeling overwhelmed? Frantic? At your wit's end? Stop, take a deep breath, and trust that there is someone available to help lessen your burden.

6. Friendships Are Precious

The older we get, the more effort it takes to maintain friendships, and yet the more important they become to our lives. Having friends is one of the main ways we continue to grow and experience ourselves as independent, individual women. Friendships are wonderful ways for us to experience ourselves as women, not only as mothers and wives. With our peers we can share our worries and concerns and receive in return love and support that helps us keep our lives in perspective. When you know two or three of your friends are also struggling to juggle their very busy lives, you might feel better able to juggle your own life.

Friendships don't just happen; they require not exactly work but commitment and nurturing. Most of us understand that a mother's life is busy and hectic, and it's always difficult to make time to see friends, chat on the phone, or e-mail a quick hello. But when too much time goes by, or too many dates have been cancelled, someone will end up with hurt feelings.

The plain truth is that sometimes friendships last and sometimes they don't. Hopefully we can all count at least one or two that have stood the test of time, weathering changes, moves outside the neighborhood or state, and arguments and disagreements. Regardless of hurt feelings or distance, you should always try to stay connected because friendships are worth it.

I have one friend who always waits for me to initiate contact. I am always the one to call, to suggest getting together, to send the Christmas or birthday card. I treat her as special because our friendship goes back to our young childhood, and I know, regardless of how much work the friendship requires and how unreciprocated it feels, that I still value our friendship. I know she has stresses in her life that prohibit her from initiating our getting together, and she always claims she doesn't want to "bother me." When I do call her, she doesn't return my calls right away, but I continue to make the effort because once we are together we talk for hours and the friendship is very mutual. We talk about our kids, our marriages, and our lives. We share feelings about getting older, look back at how we've changed and ahead to dreams we have of futures that don't include dependent kids. We are friends. We share our lives, and in this sharing, my life feels enriched and more meaningful.

Does it bother me that she relies on me to do all the so-called work of the relationship? Yes. But I know that if I didn't make the effort, we wouldn't have a friendship.

Growing a Circle of Friends

Just as it is important to maintain friendships with people we've known over time, it's also important to remain open to making new friends. Doing so requires that you put yourself out there, but it's worth it in the end. When I come into a new situation, like my kids going to high school, I go out of my way to introduce myself to other parents and extend a social invitation or suggest a get-together. When my middle son started playing football, I asked some of the other "football parents," whom we often sat with during games, if they wanted to go out to dinner. And last year Jim and I offered to throw a party as an auction item for our kids' school. A group of parents I didn't know bought our party, and I met many new people from my kids' school. Ever since the party I have made a conscious effort to stay in touch with them, inviting them to a mother-daughter Christmas ornament exchange, as well as other functions, and it pleases me to see my circle of friends grow.

Meeting new people is a constant reminder of the wide world in which we live, and the older we get and more set in our ways we become, it's easier to close ourselves off from the new. We become so enmeshed in our lives that we cease to look outside the bubbles we create around our kids, school, and established friends in our social circles. And when we cut ourselves off from new experiences, especially the experience of meeting new people, we stunt our experience of ourselves. Again, friendships—new or old—enrich our lives.

Stay at Home or Work Outside the Home: A Moot Controversy

Whether you are a working mom or a stay-at-home mom, life is stressful, difficult, and presents its own unique challenges. As a stay-at-home mom, I feel that I do anything but stay at home. I carpool, do errands, shop for the family, volunteer. My days are full, and often I wish there was an office I could go to just to escape. Like so many women who gave up careers to be at home full-time with their kids, it's stressful and difficult to always feel good about what I'm doing. I get bored; I get resentful. It takes a conscious effort to check in with myself and make sure I keep my job in perspective so I don't get too absorbed in my children's lives at the expense of my own life or my relationships.

And yet I know there are plenty of women who would rather be in my shoes. I have many friends who are working moms and envy my being able to see more of my kids on a daily basis. At the same time, they admit that they value their jobs and would find it difficult to stay at home full-time with their kids. Work makes them feel independent and self-sufficient and, they admit, better mothers. As one woman explained, "I know myself. I would go crazy if I stayed at home all day with my kids. I am a better mother when I walk in that door because I feel better about myself. Now don't get me wrong, there are days when the balancing act seems just that—an act. And I have missed some important moments in my children's lives. But I feel overall that this is the best situation for me."

These women choose to work because they enjoy the time outside the home and/or experience their work as a meaningful career. One woman, Carrie, is a lawyer. Ever since she was a small child, she knew she wanted to work in the legal field, helping others. Once she got married and started her family, she couldn't even imagine giving up her work—she felt as if a piece of her would simply wither and die. But is it hard? "Some mornings I wake up and I just don't know how I am going to find the energy to make it through the day. Weeks are a whirlwind. But I am doing the best I can do. I know that. My kids know that. My husband knows that. We are a team and we are making it work." When women work outside the home, they tend to have a lot of mixed feelings: They enjoy their jobs, but they are also torn by guilt and worry that they aren't spending enough time at home with their family.

For many women, working outside the home is less a choice and more a necessity. They are often the sole breadwinner or a major breadwinner for their family, and many dream of a day when they can stay at home with their kids.

The debate between what is best for kids—to have a mother stay at home in a traditional way or to have a mother work outside the home—is ongoing and rancorous. I also think it's a moot point. Regardless of whether a woman works outside the home to develop a career that's important to her, has to work outside the home because of financial necessity, or stays at home working full-time with and for her children, the decision is a personal choice that a woman alone can come to peace with. Instead of women from both sides of the fence being judgmental, we all should be supportive of one another's situations. Motherhood is by far one of the most challenging, demanding jobs there is. Women who work outside the home have just as hard a time as those who work at home, and vice versa. Instead of focusing on who's right and who's wrong, I'd like to see women accepting their lives as they are and helping each other become the best they can be.

7. Positive Vibes Come from Positive People

People who live in a cloud of negative energy are not good for anyone. Choosing who to hang out with is a right that comes with age. With only so many hours in any given day, we want to spend them with people who enrich our lives with positive energy.

I believe there is nothing shameful in becoming more selective with your friends and acquaintances, especially if you are gracious about it. Sure there are friends you nurse through problems or illnesses, and difficult family members you cannot—or don't want to—write off. We all have someone in our lives we want to help, though he or she seems unable to be helped—regardless of how much help you give. But in order to stay true to ourselves, we need to learn how to draw the line and separate ourselves from those people who seem to suck our spirits dry.

I had a friend who always compared herself (and everything she did) to me. When I failed in an area, she seemed to capitalize on it. She compared our children from how they were born (she made me feel inadequate because I had a C-section) to their potty training progress to how many teeth they lost. She always wanted to make herself look like a better mom with better kids. Not surprisingly, I finally and gradually stopped calling her as much. When I did call her or see her, I limited the information that I shared with her.

Eventually, our fiendship grew further and further apart.

Do I miss her? Sometimes. But to be honest, her incessant competitiveness undermined my ability to trust her as a friend, and for me, a friendship without trust breeds negative energy that whittles away at one's sense of reality. Essentially I began to feel unsettled around her. This is not to say that it's easy to pull away. How can we do this while still being kind? There's no need to openly declare war by calling or writing a note. Be gentle, and always polite, but make yourself unavailable. Often I try to focus on the positives when I'm trying to ward off a negative friend: I'll tell a glum-faced pal how great it is when she smiles or how much I enjoy her company when she is looking on the bright side of life.

If worse comes to worst, take advantage of your caller I.D. and screen your calls—and don't feel guilty about it. Optimism and enthusiasm are contagious, and we want to catch that vibe! Within reason we all have a right to protect our good spirits, because we all need them, and friends or acquaintances who threaten our positive energy are often not worth it.

Resist the Urge to Gossip

I always say that if you're on the phone more than three minutes, talk turns to gossip. Avoid it!

8. Relaxation Is the Key To Serenity

It sounds like an oxymoron, but relaxing takes work. And it's work that must be done, for the sake of peace of mind. Relaxation needs to be a priority for busy mothers, not a guilty and all-too-infrequent treat. It's important to figure out what works for us and helps us achieve a state of serenity. Then we can create rituals around the activities that we find calming and carve out the time in our lives to enjoy them. Everyone in our families benefits from this newfound energy. Use these tips to get started:

Wind down at night. Easier said than done? Perhaps, but try taking time every night to relax before going to bed. I light candles in my bathroom, and whether I have lots of time or only a few precious minutes, I take a bath to calm myself before I go to bed. In the bath I reflect on my day and prepare my body for a sound sleep. This enables me to tap into the mental and physical energy I need for the next round in the boxing ring of life.

Take time for music. Perhaps music makes you feel calm and powerful. Listen to your favorite songs using headphones and give yourself the time to close your eyes and lose yourself in the moment. Or if loud music and dancing is your thing, turn up the volume in your bedroom (with the door closed, of course!) or in your living room if you happen to be home alone—go nuts and enjoy yourself!

Do something just for you. Many people find strenuous activities like aerobics or running to be relaxing. Others enjoy the spiritual aspects of yoga or meditation. Gardening might allow your mind to roam freely, or maybe long car rides or losing yourself in a good book does it for you. I enjoy and make time for as many of these activities—in small doses—as I can. I believe that I deserve these treasured moments of serenity. You do too.

Relaxation is an undervalued art; discovering your own best path to this elusive state of grace will make you a happier woman, a more effective and loving mother, and a spouse that any man would be delighted to come home to.

Give the Gift of a Spontaneous Smile

Without ever realizing it, we can run around doing a million and one things each day with a frown on our faces. Are we unhappy? Not necessarily. Stressed? Probably. I always try and remind myself to smile—not just to keep those frown lines from burrowing their nasty selves into my forehead—but because I know that smiles are contagious. The more I smile, the better I feel, and the more others see smiles, the more likely they will smile in return.

Your Daily Life:
At Home, at Work, and in Time

9. Manage Your Time

We all have days when we just can't seem to get anything done. An obstacle meets us at every turn in the road, and by the end of the day we are exhausted and frustrated, feeling as if we got nothing done. Then there are days when everything seems to get done as if by magic. There's no traffic when we drive the kids to school, we find a parking space at the grocery store when we have to run in for one gallon of milk, and we manage to return all our phone calls. A friend of mine calls such in-sync days "Doris Day Days" because they seem effortless. So the question is, how do we increase the number of "Doris Day Days" and decrease (or banish entirely) the bad ones? Plan, plan, plan!

Keeping my priorities in mind, I maintain a master list that helps me stay organized and makes me more efficient. I write everything down on a yellow pad each morning. At the beginning of the next day, I transfer anything not done the day before to the present day. If I write it down, there is a much better chance of my doing it—whether that is returning a phone call, paying a bill, or remembering to take a walk.

When you stay organized, you get more done, and when you get more done, you feel more fulfilled, more calm, and more at peace with yourself. In this way, managing your time is an important way to take care of yourself. The woman who runs her life by the seat of her pants is sabotaging her own life by missing appointments, overextending herself, and always being late. There will be days when she will disappoint friends, family, and coworkers. Ultimately she is the loser. A good friend of mine had to learn this the hard way. She was always relaxed and easygoing by nature, which worked when she was in her twenties. She thought she could wing it the rest of her life. Once she got married, had kids, and continued working, she almost lost all three because of her lack of focus. So even though it's not easy

A Place for Everything

An easy way to increase harmony and reduce chaos in your daily life is to create a place for the important things in your life so that you don't waste any time looking for your keys, searching for your purse, or digging out your latest credit card bill. At your next opportunity, create a place for your:

Keys

Purse

Mail

Bills

Appointment book or handheld computer

(or natural, as she says) for her to sit down and make a list of all that she has to do on her handheld computer (categories: home, work, kids, self), she knows her life is working so much better now.

   Am I perfect? No. Human? Absolutely. I admit there are days when I don't want to plan a thing. I get so tired of the sheer act of applying my brain to organizing the day that I just want to close my eyes. But most days I summon the energy, and as a result, my life runs more smoothly, and I feel a lot saner more often than not.

Relax in an Instant

For me, a bath surrounded by candles offers instant relaxation. What works for you? Here are some suggestions:

Take a walk at a nearby nature reserve.

Take a drive out to the country—and don't bring your cell phone!

Go window shopping!

Take a nap.

Get a massage.

Give yourself a pedicure.

Call an old friend for a chat.

Clean out your car.

10. Be Flexible

As important as routine is for kids, it's just as important for us adults to remain flexible. If we get too married to one particular way of running our lives, we not only miss opportunities for surprises but also increase the likelihood that we will begin to experience our routine as drudgery. So in addition to being organized and getting things done, you need to be able to roll with the punches.

Typically a type A personality, I plan almost each and every minute of most days. With so much I want to get done, the only way to accomplish it all is to burn rubber and follow my list. But life sometimes gets in the way. I am thinking of a recent time when I got a call from my son's school; he had forgotten an important paper at home. My choices? Get furious at him for interrupting my day's plan or simply deliver the paper to school and go on with my day. Whatever I'm not able to get done on that day carries over to the next. This happens to us moms all the time when our kids get sick, forget their lunch, or the toilet overflows and you have to spend your morning waiting for the plumber to show up! By having a plan, I can amend it if need be; but if I have no plan to begin with, I can feel lost.

You always have two choices: Let the change get in your way and make you aggravated or simply integrate the incident into your day. The reality hasn't changed, but your peace of mind sure has.

11. Hibernate

Sometimes I declare it's time for me to hibernate. When I begin to feel physically run down, emotionally overwhelmed, or tired, I know I need a break, and I take one, two, or five days in which I don't work out, I cancel my appointments, I make only those phone calls that are absolutely necessary, or I take a daily nap—even if "nap" means closing my eyes for twenty minutes. This change in my routine gives me the rest I need and also tells everyone around me that I need time to myself. I call it, "Leave me alone week"!

Another way to take a break from your routine is by taking a mini vacation. These little holidays are a mother's way to save her sanity and give herself a much needed respite from all her worries. When our lives are so hectic and busy, it's mandatory that we put aside time to rest, relax, and recharge. That's what vacations are for. And a vacation does not mean you have to go on a faraway trip that costs a fortune. To me a vacation is any adventure, outing, or break from your daily routine that helps you unwind, leave your daily concerns and worries behind, and gives you a chance to rest and relax.

I take short trips with my mom or sisters to Chicago. Sometimes Jim and I will take a drive in the country and stay overnight at a B&B. The idea is to take a step out of your day-to-day environment and let yourself relax. Whether a block of time is 24 hours or 24 minutes, if you set aside the time with the intention of relaxation, then it's time well spent. Go to a museum. Get a manicure. Go to a movie solo.

Give yourself time for your thoughts to come to the surface. Give yourself time to cry, if you need to. And when you do, you give yourself the chance to revitalize your spirit.

Shopping as a Soothing Salve

I love to go antiquing, especially when I want to reduce stress. We have an area not far out of town that is known for its antique stores. Some of them are filled with knickknacks and junk, and somehow it calms me to spend time rummaging through these artifacts from yesteryear. Friends of mine love to go window shopping. They will spend an afternoon at the mall not so much to buy but to browse the new fashions and look at home furnishings.

12. Create a Comfortable and Inviting Home

So maybe you're not the queen of home decorating, but whether you like to fuss with furnishings or hate the thought, creating a comfortable home has the power to give you peace of mind, the very essence of what keeps you happy, centered, and engaged in your life.

Of course the definition of comfortable and inviting is in the eye of the beholder. Given the size of my family, our house is what I call indestructible. I've found that a house like mine does not have to be crammed with furniture, toys, or other extraneous objects. I try to make it both family-friendly and as serene as possible. I use muted jewel tones, such as burgundy, bronze, and gold, to minimize the visual effects of natural wear and tear. For instance, the carpet in all the bedrooms is the same bronze color, not a different color in each room, which would visually chop up the house. And the neutral color and muslin texture is low-cut and sturdy enough to hide dirt, vacuum marks, and foot tracks.

Hiding the Wear and Tear

The walls are textured with stucco so fingerprints don't show, and the floors are dark hardwood so they, too, hide dirt. To make the rooms feel more comfortable and cozy, I use a lot of area rugs. Much of the furniture has a distressed painted finish which better camouflages the inevitable nicks and damage that occur. In our first house we had white linoleum on the kitchen floor, and every time people came over, they left marks on the floor. One babysitter who came on Saturday nights left black scuff marks from her boots every week. I was a slave to cleaning the floor!

Since I spend so much of my time in my home and want it to reflect who I am, I use small details to invoke a warm, serene mood. I let the aroma of cooking and baking waft through the house—especially when the kids and my husband arrive home—and after dinner, I light scented candles and put them in high places so the younger kids can't reach them. I sometimes put one in the kitchen sink to absorb the odors from our last meal and ready the kitchen for the next! I arrange pillows and blankets on the sofas to encourage everyone to sit back and relax.

An Inviting Space

An inviting house is one that feels comfortable and puts forth a welcoming vibe to all those who visit. Pictures can work wonders and don't need to cost an arm and a leg. I collect all the kids' artwork, file most of it, and then for a Christmas gift for Jim, frame my favorite pieces and put them up in the hall or mudroom. I also frame photos—nothing is more inviting than tables or walls covered with framed snapshots of laughing people.

As long as you can wield a watering can, you can spruce up any lifeless corner with plants or flowers. And music transforms the atmosphere in a split second. Choose music to suit your mood: Infuse your home with positive energy or introduce a note of serenity.

But most of all don't be swayed by the idea of perfection: Perfect houses are not very welcoming for guests or family. And yet adding a few simple touches can turn any home into a place where family and friends—and our children's friends—want to hang out.

When we take care of our homes, we are taking care of a part of ourselves. By taking the time to create a warm, inviting home, we are letting the world around us know that we are open and welcoming, and this message creates a positive ripple that affects those who live in our home and anyone who enters it. And when we send out this message, we receive it back.

13. A Clean House Makes a Calm Home

While not everyone can afford a regular cleaning service to keep dirt and clutter from building up in our homes, we all can put aside time each week to maintain a clean and neat home. Indeed, a clean home is another way to care for ourselves and promote peace of mind. I had a friend in college who loved doing laundry. When I realized this I asked her, "Why are you so obsessed with doing the laundry?" She responded quite simply, "It calms me down. Any time I am feeling anxious or overwhelmed, I start by doing my laundry." I have always remembered her insightful words.

Though maintaining our homes is arduous and can feel like sheer drudgery, doing so has the power to create a peaceful state of mind—like taking a hot shower.

To stay organized keep a list on the refrigerator of cleaning tasks and check them off as they are done each week:
- **Wipe counters** with antibacterial soap
- **Clean out refrigerator**
- **Vacuum**
- **Dust surfaces**
- **Wipe window sills and blinds**
- **Have children clean** their own rooms, make their beds, put their clothes away each morning or each evening, and select one household chore to do.
- **Declutter your house** on a regular basis, giving away

unused toys, magazines, newspapers, and other objects that your family doesn't use.

- **Go through all closets** at the end of each season and donate clothing to a local charity or family in need.
- **Do laundry regularly** and put it away soon after it's washed and folded.

I try not to become overwhelmed by the long list of tasks but to tackle something on the list each day. Remember, this is not about having a perfect house! It's about keeping your home tidy so that your mind feels tidy! When my house looks nice, smells fresh, and feels clean to the touch, my mind clears, my mood lightens, and I am able to do more in my day.

If You Don't Use It, Lose It

You need to reassess what's in your closet on a regular basis. After each season, I go through my closet and my drawers in search of clothes I haven't worn. If a blouse, sweater, or pair of pants has gone two seasons without being on my body, then I know it's time to give it away.

14. Respect Money

We can get ourselves into deep water very quickly—with nothing solid to keep us afloat—if we don't balance our household income with our spending. Though it sounds so rational, you'd be amazed by how many families don't take this simple step.

My father taught me and my sisters a strong work ethic, based on the values that work makes you stronger and money is meant to be earned and respected. As a result, I have always found ways to earn money, put some aside, and watch my spending. But respecting money takes guts and commitment.

Remember the summer camp I ran when I was thirteen? That was one of many rather creative jobs I have had over the years. Another swashbuckler money-earning scheme was when I decided to sell my chocolate chip cookies. Not to toot my own horn, but many people had told me how delicious my cookies were. So one summer, I decided to try to sell them. Pregnant with child number eight, I approached a retailer in my nearby mall, four small kids in tow. "Would you like to sell my cookies?" I asked. She smiled politely and said, "Oh dear, no thank you." Embarrassed, I looked at her and said, "Here, take them for free. You can try them and let me know if you like them." Before she could say no, I had hightailed it out of the store.

The next day the woman called, saying the cookies were delicious. I was ecstatic! I started baking and selling the cookies for the next several months before I ran out of steam. My total earnings? One thousand dollars!

Watch Your Spending

My point in sharing this story? Regardless of how much you amass, earning money develops your respect for money and for yourself for earning it. In America, overspending and the ensuing debt are the most frequent cause of unhappiness in families. Unsolicited credit cards arrive daily in the mail, stores offer a year's deferred payment, interest rates are reasonable—there are a thousand and one reasons to spend money we don't have. But keep in mind that just because we can get hold of money in the form of credit doesn't mean it's really ours to spend. Credit is simply an expensive way to borrow.

On the other hand I'm the first to admit that beautiful things can cheer us up. Sometimes we deserve a treat. But we can only really enjoy these luxuries knowing that we are not stepping into a sinkhole because of a desire for short-term gratification.

Each month I sit down and balance my checkbook using a program such as Quicken. It may be a bore, but I know that doing so keeps me from drowning in overspending. I list all my debits and credits, and then I break down my credit card purchases into categories to see how much I spent in each area so that I can create a budget. It doesn't mean I can't have fun or be extravagant every now and then, but it does mean I won't get a nasty shock when I go to the ATM.

One life-altering task we all can do every month that has a real impact on the quality of our lives now and in the future: save. Jim's father continues to remind us to put money aside so the well doesn't run dry. So I always remember to put something aside for a rainy day—whether it's $5, $50, or $500. That way I have peace of mind that spending just can't buy.

Create a Slush Fund

Set up an automatic withdrawal from your primary checking account into a savings account. Most savings accounts offer interest, which though low, adds more incentive for saving. Just think: A year of saving $100 a month will yield $1,200 plus interest! That $1,200 could earn you more than $6,000 in five years, more than $12,000 in ten years, and almost $20,000 in fifteen years. Not bad!

15. Good Enough

How can we do more? I have spoken with hundreds of moms—some who work, some who don't—who say they are exhausted, depleted, and have nothing left to give. They function in their lives, go through their days, but without energy or joy. They feel like they are merely treading water, not actually living. So many women are juggling so many tasks, and yet they feel ill at ease and inadequate. Not because they aren't doing anything. They literally don't have time to add one more thing to their agendas. Despite so many accomplishments, despite loving their families, their kids, their husbands, their lives, they feel a sense that something is not quite right. I know this situation well because I have felt this way too.

Let me take a step back and tell you both how I got into that predicament and how I got out.

I always knew I was a good mom and that my kids were happy, healthy, well-adjusted, and finding their way through life. I knew that my husband and I had a good, solid, loving relationship, a safe home, and a hopeful future. I felt connected to my community, my extended family, and friends. On the surface, everything was perfect. I was living the life I had always wanted, always dreamed of. And yet something was nagging at me because there were times— moments, days, weeks even—when life felt overwhelming.

For years I wanted to do more. I carried this feeling around inside of me that I wasn't doing a good enough job, but I was afraid to give it too much attention. I didn't want it to grow. I didn't want to look for a solution only to find a problem bigger than I could handle or solve. And yet the feeling wouldn't go away. It would stay with me until I realized that, in fact, I am good enough.

Just Doing It

As I mentioned in the introduction, for years people have asked me how I managed to "do it all." In response I smiled politely, but at heart, I didn't really understand what they were getting at. This was my life. Sure it was a big life simply by the fact that I have so many children. But I didn't see my life as much different from those of the many other mothers' lives around me.

Yet their questions always made me think twice about the fact that yes, I am doing it all—perhaps not perfectly—but I am doing it. The more I thought about it, the more I began to make a shift in attitude from one of coping to one of acceptance, confidence, and celebration. I realized that no day was perfect, no child was perfect, and I was certainly not a perfect mother, but I always did the best I could do, and on most days, I was happy with the results: I am raising my kids, showing them how to be kind, accomplished adults. I am running a busy household, managing my family, and maintaining a loving, fruitful relationship with my husband. Then it dawned on me: Though I may not be perfect, and I certainly am not supermom, I am doing a wonderful job. I am a wonderful mother, a wonderful wife, a wonderful human being. How do I define wonderful? Good enough.

How do you shift your attitude from one of "How can I get through another day?" to "What a great day!"? Don't spend half your time being miserable and the other half telling your spouse everything you've done all day, looking for sympathy. You have to start by becoming aware of all that you do and give yourself a giant break. Then you have to give everything your all and accept that you've done your best. And finally you have to let yourself believe that all that you do is indeed good enough.

I look back at my life—my three decades of having children—and laugh. How have I done it? Changed all those diapers? Taken all those kids to school? Wiped all those runny noses? Life is easier now because of what I've learned—that I don't have to be perfect, that no one expects me to be perfect, and that supermoms are for comic strips not for real life.

Your Body, Your Self
16. Accept Your Body

It's the bane of many a mother's existence: We eat our
children's leftovers, snack when bored or unhappy, or simply
never lose the extra pounds we put on with pregnancy. And
though there are many strategies and diets that can help
women lose unwanted weight, what is more complicated is
how our thoughts and feelings about ourselves are directly
reflected by our behavior toward food and eating. Simply put,
a negative attitude toward food (such as feeling that it controls
us, not the other way around) takes away our confidence and
belittles our self-esteem. And it's this shaky belief in oneself
that is at the root of many a real weight problem.

Unfortunately I have seen how perilous a negative attitude
toward food can be. As a teenager, one of my best friends
became anorexic. She became so obsessed about how she
looked, what foods she ate, and what she weighed, she
could no longer eat. At one time my beautiful 5'4" friend
weighed only 77 pounds. She was so thin she had to be
hospitalized, put on intravenous nourishment, and
monitored for more than a month. Then followed years of
therapy and counseling.

While eating disorders such as anorexia and bulimia never
have just one cause, any kind of disordered eating—eating
too little or too much—is exacerbated by our society's
obsession with looking thin and beautiful. We are assaulted

each day by the media with images of women in thin, ageless, perfect bodies that are always airbrushed! We internalize these images and hold them up as unnerving comparisons that we cannot possibly emulate. The result? Again, our self-confidence diminishes.

Thankfully, my dear friend fully recovered from her eating disorder. She worked long and hard, examining the underlying causes of what was driving her to limit her food intake to such a dramatic degree. Regardless of whether we have an eating problem, it's healthy for all of us to look at our relationships with food for hidden clues to our selves. For instance, I had to stop seeing food as a reward or a comfort and take it for what it is: necessary sustenance for survival. If we think of food not as our enemy but as that which nourishes us, food will begin to lose its power. But for some people, shifting their attitude toward food from negative to positive requires deep emotional examination. My dear friend taught me this lesson: You don't get anorexia or bulimia because you want to be thin like a model. Rather controlling food intake in drastic measures is a way to control an emotional problem you have not resolved.

Avoid Impossible Goals

I believe it's a worthy goal to be fit and look good in your body, but I think it's equally important—if not more important—to keep in mind that weight is not the real issue: A positive self-image along with high self-esteem is what is most important. No one needs to be as skinny as the runway models, and most of the men in our lives wouldn't want us to look like that anyway! Why drive ourselves crazy with impossible goals? We need to respect how our bodies are shaped. Some of us are naturally tall and thin. Others are more round—round hips, round legs, round tummies. Others are more square. Your ideal weight depends on your genetically determined bone structure, height, and body size. Once you are happy with yourself, you will accept your body type. Then you can focus on whether you want to lose weight, maintain your weight, or even gain weight.

Getting Help

If you are suffering from an eating disorder, do not despair. You can get help by reaching out to a professional. Just like alcoholism, an eating disorder can affect the whole family. Consult the National Eating Disorders Association (www.nationaleatingdisorders.org) for a referral near you.

17. Be Wary of Fad Diets

Many of the popular diets that promise to help you lose weight are often based on inaccurate and misleading information: Many claim that some foods have special properties that can cause weight loss or gain. They tend to restrict foods, which often leads to cravings for foods that are not on the diet. Once a person gives in to a craving, she tends to throw the diet out the window. Yo-yo dieting—going on a diet and off again, and back on again—is not only unhealthy for our bodies but also our brains. It reinforces a lack of confidence when it comes to being able to control eating behavior.

I maintain my weight by eating in moderation. I like to graze throughout the day, eating smaller portions or mini meals. But I always try to eat enough to feel sated. Many people eat so quickly and so much they don't give their bodies time to realize they are already full, or they eat so little they go around hungry most of the day and then gorge at night. To maintain a healthy weight it's important to eat enough food to keep your body from feeling hungry.

Losing Weight

If you want to lose weight, cut your starchy carbohydrates (bread and pasta), walk away from the empty calories found in junk food or sugar, avoid caffeine, and drink lots of water daily. And remember: Keep your refrigerator filled with healthy foods, especially fresh fruits and vegetables, and get rid of the junk food. How are you supposed to resist the cookies, chips, or coffee cake if it's right in front of you?

Find a buddy to train with or get yourself an MP3 player for some extra motivation at the gym. Exercise definitely helps the pounds disappear because it increases your ability to burn calories. It also tones your body and gives you more energy.

The American Dietetic Association, which evaluates all diets for health and success, suggests that "successful weight loss (which means both losing the weight and keeping it off for at least five years) is accomplished by making positive changes to both eating habits and physical activity patterns." Here's their general advice:

- **Get moving!** Establish a pattern of regular physical activity, start slowly, and gradually increase duration and intensity.
- **Try weight lifting.** Weight lifting increases muscle mass, and muscle uses more calories than fat.
- **Eat a wide variety of foods.** Your body needs nutrients from all the food groups—complex carbohydrates, protein, and fat. Your body's main source of energy comes from carbohydrates, so most of your diet should be made up of carbs—but choose whole grains, vegetables, and fruits, all of which contain lots of fiber. Also stay away from processed carbs, which give many people cravings.
- **Tailor your portion sizes.** Restaurants in this country have redefined the size of a healthy portion, often doubling what authorities recommend. The right amount of food per serving should fit in the palm of your hand.
- **If you want to diet**, chose one that is realistic, easy for you to follow, and compatible with your family's lifestyle.

18. The Wondrous Power of Sleep

Grant yourself the gift of getting enough rest. Personally I can't function well when I'm running on empty, and I don't think anyone can. Most people nowadays operate on too little sleep, thinking it's the best way to get everything crammed into their hectic schedules. But pause for a moment and think: Does your car work well when it's low on oil? Not for long.

I need at least seven hours of sleep each night. If I don't get it, I'm cranky, quick tempered, and scattered. When I'm unable to focus well, I become less efficient, less happy, and eventually I just fall apart, exhausted. This is how important sleep is to me.

Though everyone's sleep requirements vary, the average person needs seven to eight hours a night. Some people may feel fine on six hours, while other people need as much as ten hours a night. But as the Better Sleep Council points out, "It's a safe bet that if you sleep longer on weekends than you do during the week, you aren't meeting your personal sleep requirements."

Sophia Loren's Beauty Secret

Getting enough sleep is necessary for proper functioning of our brains and our bodies. But most important, it's crucial for staying emotionally intact. Did you know that sleep deprivation is the most effective form of torture? It wears people down psychologically. And over time we react to loss of sleep in similar ways. To be effective, happy, and full of energy we need those magic Zzz's. But how?

You may be thinking there just aren't enough hours in the day for the sleep you need, but that's not so. You can steal extra time. If your kids are old enough to drink from cups, for instance, they can get up on a weekend morning and make their own breakfast (lay it out for them the night before). During the day I create a "quiet time" rule for little ones during which they read and draw in their rooms.

When I can't nap I sit quietly by myself or close my eyes for five or ten minutes while waiting in the car to pick up the kids. I also sleep at my hair appointment under the dryer or in the waiting room at the doctor's office. And I always try to remember that sleep is Sophia Loren's beauty secret.

Here are some other ideas:

- **Turn off the TV** at night and sleep instead.
- **Take turns** with your husband to sleep in or go to bed early.
- **Use a fan** or noise machine to drown out ambient sound.
- **Every now and then** treat yourself to a nap. Even if you can't fall asleep in the middle of the day, the rest will do wonders for relaxing you. And the more relaxed you are, the better you will sleep at night.
- **If you have trouble falling asleep**, don't lie in bed fidgeting. Get up and go somewhere comfortable to read. Return to bed once you are sleepy.
- **Don't drink caffeine** after midday, and don't replace sleep

with a cup of coffee! The coffee will steal your energy when it wears off, and it will steal your sleep later that night.

Remember the powerful sense of possibility and the boundless energy you feel when you've had a wonderful night's sleep? Let's make it a priority to recharge ourselves in this way more often. Sleeping is not wasting time; it allows us to tackle the world, day after day, with full hearts and healthy bodies.

19. Exercise for Everyone

One of the most important ways I take care of myself is by staying physically fit. Working out is my solace, my health insurance, and my special time each day. In short, you could say that exercise is the method to my madness. And although I have always been athletic and have enjoyed sports, I know that not all women are like me. But I do know that all women—regardless of their body type, weight, or athletic inclination—feel better about themselves when they exercise regularly. The challenge is finding the time, deciding what's right for you, doing it, and sticking to it.

When I first ran my Boot Camp, an exercise and weight lifting class I offer from my home, the ladies said they dreaded coming. But after just one week, they paid me in advance to make sure they didn't miss it. Before they started working out, they couldn't imagine how good it would feel. Now they want to know when I'm having my next one!

Make a Routine

The key is to make your particular exercise part of your weekly routine. At the beginning of each week, look ahead to what you have going on. Which days are most likely to be workout days? Tuesday and Thursday? Mark that time on your calendar/agenda. By writing it down, you are more likely to consider your exercise a "must do" item. If, on the other hand, you don't take the mental step to actually fit exercise into your schedule ahead of time, it's unlikely that exercise will become a reality. Another tip is to put on your workout clothes when you get dressed in the morning to remind you to work out.

Say you begin walking two miles two days a week. You will begin to feel better in two weeks. Guaranteed. And think of it this way: At the end of three months, you can say to yourself that you walked more than 50 miles. Imagine that!

20. Pumping Iron Is for Regular Women

Jim got me into weight lifting because he showed me how it gives the best results in the shortest amount of time: Weight lifting keeps me toned and lean, and it increases my muscle mass, which in turn burns more calories. I work out four days out of seven and change my routine every 6 to 8 weeks. It only takes 30 minutes, so it's not like it requires a lot of time. You can begin with any size weight that's comfortable, but you should probably begin slowly and gradually increase the weight. Here's my routine:

On Monday I do biceps and chest.

On Tuesday I workout my legs.

On Thursday I focus on my shoulders and triceps.

On Friday I work on my back muscles.

Weight lifting is simple and doesn't require a lot of expense or room. You can work with a couple sets of dumbbells. Or join a gym. Most gyms, including Ys, have excellent equipment. If you can, sign up for a couple of sessions of instruction. And as always, be careful when you start—take it slowly and build up gradually.

Adding Cardio

I also add four days of cardio workouts (either walking or running on the treadmill, using the stair stepper, or riding the stationary bike) for at least twenty minutes, and do abdomen and butt exercises *(see box, below)* each of the four weight lifting days. It's the combination of increasing muscle (through weight training) and burning calories (through cardio) that keeps me in shape.

My Firm Fanny Exercise

This routine will not only reduce the size of your derriere, it will also keep it more elevated.

- Get on all fours.

- Raise one leg at a time and point your foot toward ceiling. Point for 50 counts, flex for 50 counts.

- Turn your hip out and repeat, pointing for 50 counts, flexing for 50 counts.

- Kick your foot toward back wall for 100 counts.

- Repeat with the other leg.

- Lie down on your back, lift one leg up, then the other for 100 reps.

21. Play a Sport

Many adults think of organized sports as just for kids and athletes. Well, we shouldn't! Tapping into our instinctive desire to win can be a great thing for our minds and our bodies.

A 40-something woman I know just started to play tennis again after a fifteen-year hiatus. Although she had played a lot of tennis as a young person, she got back into the game by taking some lessons, participating in clinics, and playing in an organized club tournament. She admitted that at first it was tough—both physically and mentally—but once she was playing more regularly (once or twice a week), she began to feel so much better about herself. "A part of me just came alive again!" she said.

Team Up

If the gym is too boring or your lifestyle too sedentary, competitive sports might just be your ticket out of couch potato heaven. Better yet, perhaps there's a sport you can play competitively with your spouse and kids. A little competition in the family is great for the soul!

Of course the heart-pumping, health-promoting benefits of any strenuous physical activity go without saying. But "group" exercise is also beneficial to our social lives, whether we forge a relationship with the parents of our children's friends or other members of the community. Team activities are motivating and reenergizing. Learning to work together with others makes us feel much more connected to the world outside the confines of our own homes and families, and this energy revitalizes us.

If you played basketball years ago, consider organizing a regular pickup game with your old cohorts. Volunteer to coach lacrosse or soccer at your local grade school or high school—this has the added benefit of giving you an insight into the world in which your children operate. Hook up with novice runners or walkers at your local gym and work toward competing together in a 5K or 10K race. I play tennis and volleyball and thrive on the competition and camaraderie!

Try Something New

If you're feeling adventurous, try something totally new. Try kickboxing or join a beginners bowling team. When you have others sweating by your side, your stamina and determination may surprise you. It can be a great thrill.

Have you ever thought about joining a volleyball team or taking up rowing or kayaking? You don't have to run long distance to benefit from a walking or jogging routine. There are plenty of sports to play and enjoy at all levels, and it's never too late to try.

Once you find a sporting activity to take part in regularly, you might just rediscover your competitive side, which is not such a bad thing. As mothers we don't want to become too nice or complacent: it's so bland. A little intensity and passion stirs us up. Also, believe me, the adrenaline rush of crushing a competitor—or giving it your best shot—beats the stair stepper any day.

22. Trust Your Own Style

The key to feeling comfortable in our own bodies—and in our clothes—is figuring out what suits us in terms of body shape, personality, and age and then establishing our own style within these guidelines. Once a woman knows her own style, she can walk with her head high, a brisk step in her gait, and, most important, her heart pounding in the center of her chest.

I've always been a T-shirt and jeans kind of gal myself. When low slung hipster jeans came into fashion, I found a pair that were low enough to be fashionable without exposing my lower half to the world. The key is to find a clothing style that flatters us without making us look foolish in our middle age. Boob-tubes don't cut it with the over-40 crowd, but an asymmetrical look could work. None of us wants to enter the land of comfortable shoes and blue-rinsed perms too early in life, but we definitely don't want to invite snickering behind our backs when we push the envelope a bit too far!

Adapt Fashion Styles to Suit You

Fashion magazines are gorgeous and fun to pore over, but we mustn't become slaves to them, nor to the opinions of our cute and skinny teenage daughters. Current trends may be fun, but they don't always work for those over the legal drinking age. Adapting fashion styles to our own personal visions of beauty is the key to accepting ourselves wholeheartedly and radiating inner confidence.

Here are some general fashion tips to consider for busy moms.

First, dress for comfort:

- Choose clothes that are easy to clean. I think you know why: Kids are messy.
- Wear clothes that are comfortable and easy to move in. You will feel so much more free!
- Select clothes that fit and flatter your body. Again, honor your shape with clothes that enhance your features rather than expose your flaws.
- Don't choose clothes that are too revealing. Exposed midriffs, low-cut blouses, and fanny-hugging skirts are not sexy; they are tacky.

Second, resist trends and fashions that quickly go out of style. Instead:

- Purchase separates that mix and match well—a couple of pairs of stylish jeans, colorful T-shirts, a few easy-to-wear blouses, and a couple of sweaters are some basics for busy moms.
- Combine hip elements with something more classic—a frilly blouse with black pants or a peasant skirt with a simple jewel-neck top.
- Mix stronger colors with neutrals to brighten your outfit and your day.

Third, add your unique touch:

- Don't be afraid to accessorize. Use a colorful belt, jazzy earrings, or a scarf to accent your outfit.
- Find a hat that works for those rushed mornings. My favorite is a baseball cap, but there are many hat styles that

can work, including a beret or a soft cowboy hat.

• Wear nice lingerie—just for you. Whether you like white cotton or black and slinky, you will feel so good knowing you're wearing something nice underneath.

Focus on enhancing your assets and trusting your style, in lieu of buying into short-term fashion trends. You want clothes to reflect your personality and mood—whether idiosyncratic, flirty, or no-nonsense—but they must also flatter our bodies and suit our personalities.

23. Keep Up with Beauty Basics

Sometimes it takes a village to look good. Most of us know how we can look our best, so often it's a question of finding the time to address what I call "beauty basics."

I like to look good but I don't like to spend a lot of time each morning—and I certainly don't have the time for an elaborate beauty ritual! I start each day by taking a quick shower and moisturizing my skin—my favorites lotions are lavender and grapeseed body butter. I like to smell good and always wear lotions with scents that are fresh and soft. Since I don't want to dry out my hair, I don't wash it every day, which actually makes it easier to style. I wear my hair down to my shoulders or up in a ponytail. As I said, I am a T-shirt and jeans kind of gal, so that's my typical wardrobe—with cowboy boots in the winter and flip-flops in the summer. But I would say that my basic beauty routine is about maintaining myself: I never let my hair go too long without a cut; I always take care of my skin and teeth; and I make sure that I get enough exercise and sleep.

Maintain Yourself

As you think about your beauty routine, consider how well you maintain yourself. Remember it's important not to let too much time pass before getting another haircut, coloring your hair, or having a manicure and pedicure. These important beauty treatments make women look and feel better, and when we look and feel better about the outside, we automatically feel better on the inside.

When I'm at the hairdresser, I always make an appointment for the next visit—if I have to cancel, at least I know I am due for that trim or color. I also love to treat myself to a manicure and pedicure every month. In between I paint my own nails and try and keep them neat and trim.

In the best of all worlds, beauty treatments would be a monthly indulgence. But if you can't afford the frills, find a talented friend who might help you do your nails or color your hair—and then return the favor. After a shower you can use scented baby oil to keep your skin smooth and fresh smelling. Once a month, put leave-in conditioner on your hair—homemade or store-bought—and wrap it up in a warm towel for super-smooth locks. For special occasions request gift certificates for massages, facials, or manicures and pedicures.

When it comes to beauty, the details are what make the overall package irresistible. Just because it takes some work to look lovely doesn't mean the effort isn't worth it. If you look good, you'll feel great, and that pleasure principle will make you shine—inside and out.

24. Pregnancy— Do It Your Way

Pregnant women experience a lot of pressure to do everything right: gain the right amount of weight; choose the best doctor; decide on the right delivery style; buy the most chic baby clothes and equipment; and so on. The pregnancy "to do" list is endless—if you let it be. How do you weather the months of anticipation without losing your head and getting carried away with doing everything right? Simply stay focused on what's right for you.

Staying Excited

I love being pregnant. I know some women might think I'm crazy. But I truly enjoy being pregnant—and it's not because I get away scot-free. I've had my share of nausea, headaches, exhaustion, and throbbing legs. At this point I know that each pregnancy changes my body and my state of mind, so I don't get caught up in fighting the tide. I know the bad days will be soon be followed by good days and that the months when a child is growing inside of me is a magical, special time that can never be replaced. So even when I'm not feeling 100 percent, I stay focused on the reason behind the massive transformations that my body is making: the baby growing inside.

If I don't feel attractive or am unable to bend or feel absolutely spent, I put my hands on my stomach and try to feel the baby inside. I get lost in thoughts about our baby to be and remind myself how special and blessed it is to be pregnant.

Having a baby is about you, the baby, your husband, and the rest of your family. If you are pregnant with your first, you're probably reading all the pregnancy magazines and books. I'm sure your doctor or midwife has advised you on how to eat, dress, and take care of your body. Essentially you have all the information you need. Now it's time for you to stay in tune with what you need to do to feel comfortable, healthy, and excited. There is plenty of time to worry and plan for your baby's future. Pregnancy is the time to ready yourself—emotionally, physically, and spiritually—for the new life that is going to arrive—sooner or later.

Personal Decisions

One of my friends told me this story, a lesson in making personal decisions. "All I wanted was one of those co-sleepers so that my baby could sleep in a bassinet near my bed. When I told my mother and sister what I wanted for a shower gift, they both said in unison, 'No way. You will not want that baby near you at night.' I listened to them and got a regular bassinet. And of course, when my daughter was born, all I wanted was for her to be near me. I ended up bringing her into my bed, where she still is, three years later!"

To me, this story is about listening to your own voice. My friend knew intuitively that she would want to be physically close to her baby. Her sister and mother probably preferred to have their babies not so close. Is there a right or wrong here? No. It's about what works for you and your baby.

When I tell people that I have never nursed a baby, they are frequently surprised. In this day and age, doctors, midwives, and many other mothers themselves pressure women to breastfeed. I can't think of a more personal decision. What's best for me has always been feeding my babies formula from a bottle. This way my husband and older kids can feed the baby, I get back into the swing of things more quickly and easily, I know my baby is growing strong and healthy just like all his siblings before him, and we are bonding beautifully. These decisions are yours to make, so research your options, think about what is best for you and your family, and make your own decision.

25. Fit Pregnancy—From Beginning to End

It's as important to stay fit during pregnancy as it is before and after pregnancy. It amazes me how many women associate getting pregnant with a free ticket to put on weight and stop exercising. Nothing could be worse for you—and your baby.

Science shows that the more fit a woman is going into pregnancy, the more fit she will remain throughout her pregnancy. Indeed, studies show that if your body is used to working out regularly, it will interpret pregnancy as one long, sustained workout! The key is staying in your workout routine during the three trimesters as you begin to tire, get bigger, and eventually slow down. Continue doing activities you were doing before you were pregnant and consult your doctor before starting anything new.

Adapt Your Routine

I definitely adapt my workout routine throughout the course of my pregnancy, but I always remain active. In my first trimester when I tend to get morning sickness and fatigue hits, I continue my weight training but modify my routine. In my second trimester when the nausea subsides and my energy returns, I reinstate my aerobic activity and play tennis as often as I can. Throughout each trimester I watch my heart rate so it doesn't get too high. In my last pregnancy, I was still playing tennis in my seventh month!

Once I get to the third trimester, I slow down. I take leisurely walks, make sure I stay limber with easy forward bends, and continue to lift weights but at lighter weights. I don't push myself as hard when pregnant, but I always do some kind of exercise because working out makes me feel sane as I grow bigger and bigger. I also know that the better shape I am in throughout my pregnancy, the easier it will be to get back into shape after the baby arrives.

Remember the better shape you are in going into a pregnancy, the easier it will be for you to maintain a workout routine during your pregnancy. However it's important for every woman to honor her body. Pregnancy is not the time, for instance, to start weight lifting or running. If you haven't yet gotten into a regular exercise routine, but want to be active during your pregnancy, try walking or a pregnancy yoga class. Both options are good for beginners and will yield wonderful results that will strengthen your body as you strengthen the baby inside of you.

Maternity Wardrobes: You Don't Have to Lose Your Style

I don't change my style just because I'm pregnant. And nowadays with Target selling Liz Lange and Isaac Mizrahi jeans, tops, and pants and other stylish and comfortable maternity clothes, you don't have to resort to wearing giant tent dresses and your husband's overalls. Pea in the Pod is one of my favorite stores for maternity clothes.
I've also taken a favorite pair of jeans and put a panel of fabric at the waistband so I could continue to wear them through most of my pregnancy. It's fashionable to be sexy throughout your pregnancy, so take advantage of the reasonably priced, easy-to-wear maternity clothes.

Let the Spirit Move You
26. Nurturing the Spirit

Though I don't wear my spirituality on my sleeve, I consider
myself a deeply spiritual person. I pray daily—with my family
and my husband, and on my own. What do I mean by
praying? Sometimes I sit in church and pray for God's many
blessings. Other days, I take a walk around a beautiful pond,
my two youngest at my side. Some days I consciously give
back to the world that has been so good to me. On other
days I take a ride out to a beautiful, serene Carmelite
Monastery and visit its chapel to pray to the Blessed
Sacrament. Prayer can happen anywhere, in whatever place
or setting that makes you feel good and closer to God or your
spirit center.

Any time I connect with what I call my spirit center I
feel as if I have prayed, in the truest sense of the word.
Staying open to this part of myself adds both strength and
meaning to my life. When a woman has her own spirit
center—however she defines it—she feels stronger and more
able to handle whatever comes her way. She feels more joy
when things are happy and better equipped to cope when
things go awry. As I like to say, "Talk to God; God listens.
God talks; we listen."

27. Stay Positive— One Day at a Time

Being happy and having an optimistic outlook on life is as much a choice as it is a genetic trait. Granted science tells us that some people have more serotonin, a brain chemical that helps people feel emotionally balanced, in their brains than others. This may account for a tendency for some to experience low moods (or depression). But I believe that we can conquer even this biological tendency by harnessing the power of a positive outlook.

No one can be happy every minute of every day. I have my share of down days, in which I seem to wallow in my sorrows, feeling sorry for myself. But I make myself focus on the small, simple things that I can do each day. I try to keep my focus on the here and now so I don't get overwhelmed by the big picture.

Using Prayer

Prayer often helps me stay positive when life seems to feel too big and unmanageable. For instance when I was named president of the hospital board, I soon felt overwhelmed by the time commitment, number of meetings, and huge responsibility of making decisions that affected so many lives. I didn't want to quit, but I knew I had to approach this job in a different way if I was going to stick it out and make it meaningful. I began to pray for patience and the ability to focus on one task at a time. The more I prayed, the more positive I felt about the job; the more positive I felt, the more my confidence grew.

When you catch yourself in a bad mood, ask yourself, "Why do I feel this way?" Is it because your husband left in the morning without saying good-bye? Is it because you are physically and mentally tired because you haven't slept through the night in you can't remember how many nights? Is it because you feel sluggish and unattractive?

Once you identify the why, it becomes much easier to keep your negative feeling from spreading and contaminating your entire being. If you feel disheartened and trace the cause of this feeling to your kids' having been unruly and disobedient, it's easier to keep that feeling in check. Then you remember that feelings always pass and you'll start to feel better.

It's very easy to get caught up in negative emotions, and they seem to have an insidious power to poke their heads into every cell of our bodies. But we can learn to keep them at bay and help develop more positive feelings.

28. Be a Strong Woman with a Soft Heart

There is strength in vulnerability. This is another lesson I have had to learn again and again. One Halloween, one of my sons got into a fight with a boy from school. Both kids were at fault, and no one was seriously hurt. However, that was not the end of the matter. The boy's mother called me that night to tell me some very unkind things about our family. I was both upset and furious by her remarks. This woman had been very insulting, as well as downright mean. And while part of me wanted to lash out and defend my children, part of me knew it might be better to take a deep breath and assess the situation further.

My family and I see this family every day at school, and I knew that if I upheld the unkindness, matters between the two families would only grow more uncomfortable. So I swallowed my pride: I called the boy's family on Thanksgiving and left a message wishing them a Happy Thanksgiving. I also reiterated my apologies for my son's having done anything to upset their child.

Having a Soft Heart

In my heart I knew I didn't owe them an apology, but I also knew I had to be the bigger heart—for all our sakes. And with my actions came a gift: The burden was lifted off my heart.

Having a soft heart means you are ready to feel another's

pain. It means you are willing to offer comfort, reach across the table and forgive, and continue to grow inside. A soft heart is that quality that enables women to love their children all the time even though they may not like their children's behaviors a lot of the time. It's the ability to be vulnerable, to acknowledge your own weaknesses or mistakes, and forgive yourself. Having a soft heart also means forgiving others for slights or hurts so you are not held back by holding grudges against others or blaming others for your hurt feelings. Most of all having a soft heart means you are always ready to move on and not linger in a place where you might feel sorry for yourself. Indeed when our hearts remain soft and open, we are living in the place of the soul.

29. Acknowledge Your Blessings

My life is full of blessings. I have ten healthy children and a wonderful marriage to a man I love. I am physically, emotionally, and spiritually strong. For this and more, I thank God on a daily basis.

Whether or not you believe in God, you can still acknowledge the good in your life. Why? Because acknowledging the good means you don't take anything for granted. It means you regard the good in your life as important, and, in doing so, it grows in significance. Good begets good. The more good in your life, the more good will grow.

30. Give Back

Many of us have blessed lives: I often marvel at the love and dedication I enjoyed growing up and the support and care I get from family and friends now. As my mother-in-law always says, "To whom much is given, much is expected." But not everyone is so fortunate, and this is where we can make a difference to others. Giving without expecting something in return is remarkably nourishing to the spirit.

Donating

Time is not such a barrier—we have more time than we think; it's a matter of what is important to us. Making time to help people outside our own families sets a great example for our children, and it also keeps us connected to the world outside our own orbit. As busy mothers it's very easy to get consumed by all our tasks, deadlines, and goals. By making a point to give to others—of your time, money, or belongings—you force yourself to remember that the world is a big place and you are not at its center. I learned this lesson as a child from my parents, and now I have role models in both my parents and Jim's parents, who continue to teach the importance of giving back each and every day. You can pass this trait on to your children as well.

Like most women, I have to make a conscious effort to remember to give back by making it part of the plan for my day, week, or month. I make a contribution to a charity, take some clothes, toys, or canned goods by a shelter or food pantry, or volunteer. First, choose a charity or organization that is meaningful to you and then figure out a way to contribute. Before motherhood, were you a businesswoman? Perhaps you could offer to write a grant for a nonprofit organization. Or do some office work for a local shelter. Do you love to read or write? You can volunteer to work in a school for underprivileged children. Even if you were not a professional or are doubtful of your abilities, helping those with less is a great first step in rediscovering your own talents.

Giving back also means asking someone if they need help. If you notice an older person trying to make his way across a busy intersection, ask him if he'd like your arm to balance him. If you see an older woman struggling to push her cart around the grocery store, maybe she would welcome your assistance.

Involve Your Children

If you can involve your children in your endeavors, so much the better. Children learn by example: I like to share stories from the newspapers and experiences from real life with my older kids. In the same vein, you could take your children with you to read to a Head Start program or serve food at a homeless shelter once a month. Encouraging them to give some of their pocket money or their gifts to the needy will make them less materialistic. At Christmastime, my kids love to pick out a gift for a child their age and donate it to a local Adopt-a-Family organization. One of my kids thought he had been paid too much for a job, so he turned around and gave a portion of his earnings to a charity of his choosing. Again, children learn from our example.

Establishing a pattern of philanthropy is the key. As you know, children learn not only by example but through repetition. So I try to be consistently generous with both my time and energy, as well as with my pocketbook. The world is a better place, thanks in some small part to our efforts. And, really, it's our duty to give something back to this world that has been so good to us.

Your Marriage

In this chapter

Overwhelmed? Don't be. Read one of these brief reflections each day, or use the following list as a guide so you can dip in and out of the book whenever you need a little advice or inspiration.

Your Marriage

One of the best compliments my husband, Jim, and I ever receive is when people say, "Are you newlyweds?" Perceiving us in this way means that Jim and I are visibly happy enjoying each other's company. And while we do have wonderful chemistry and share many interests in common, we are nowhere near the beginning of our relationship. In fact we met 25 years ago and have been married nineteen years—much to our own amazement at times. At the heart of what makes our marriage work so well is the deep, abiding care each of us takes for the other and our relationship as a whole. Yes some of marriage is work. But it shouldn't be work that is strenuous, exhausting, or depleting. Rather when two people love each other, share the same values, can laugh and joke together, and enjoy each other's company like best friends, they should also be able to weather the storms any relationship can bring. And that means creating the kinds of ties that bind. I believe a relationship needs to have three different types of bonds in order to stay healthy and thrive. A couple needs to relate emotionally, physically, and spiritually.

All three of these dimensions must be nurtured and acknowledged in order for two people to stay connected in a relationship.

- **Attraction.** It's common for couples to have some very strong physical periods when romance is very alive and electric. The two of you feel passionate and attracted to each other.

- **Friendship.** Then there are other times when the pulse of passion wanes. You still feel very close, but more as friends. This emotional connection is central to your relationship and your family. As friends two committed partners can have fun, comfort each other, argue, and make up. It's this bond that helps ground the two of you in life and gives your relationship longevity.
- **Spiritual connections.** These are more elusive and harder to define, but they remain a crucial way that couples stay deeply joined at the core of their beings. When two people connect spiritually, they allow their souls to feel as one. In the bustle of day-to-day life it's difficult to tap into this ephemeral dimension, but it's not impossible and it's very important.

Life is fast and full—so we don't always relate to each other in these three ways all at once. But when a couple develops all three of these bonds, they infuse each other and their family with love, energy, and hopefulness, and give their relationship depth, meaning, and purpose beyond the here and now.

Born of my own experiences—and, yes, mistakes—the 30 reflections that follow offer practical advice to help you and your spouse communicate better, insight into how you can love each other more deeply and openly, and inspiration to take your union to a deeper, more soulful place, moving your relationship from the realm of the ordinary to the extraordinary. Think of it as the next step in your journey of true, lasting love.

Staying in Tune and Attached

1. Be Friends

Although couples often start out primarily as lovers, it's the friendship dimension of our relationship that has the sturdiest legs. I met Jim at a party when I was 16 and he was 17. From the minute I saw him, I was very physically attracted to him. I remember sitting on his lap and that he was wearing a cowboy hat. It didn't take long before we were hanging out. Yes we were typical childhood sweethearts, but I knew we were also best friends. How did I know? We loved spending time together, we shared many interests and values, and we laughed—a lot! As my mother loves to remind me, she always knew when it was Jim on the phone because I was laughing.

It's now 25 years later and he and I are still best friends, and I am still laughing! We workout together, play tennis together, and attempt to play golf together. We make coffee dates during the week, squeeze in a lunch date, or take drives to get ice cream—just the two of us.

This strong friendship is the core of our relationship. What is a friendship? A relationship between two people based on mutual interests, camaraderie, and respect. When two people enjoy each other's company, look forward to seeing each other, and miss each other when separated, they are friends.

Jim is always the one to whom I turn to share my thoughts—

however trivial—whether it's good news or bad news. For instance when Oprah called about wanting our family to be featured in her magazine, I waited until Jim got home to listen to her message together. I wanted him beside me as we shared the fantastic news together. Why? He's my best friend.

Being in love forever depends on being friends forever. When two people are kind, thoughtful, and considerate of each other, when they pick up slack and give each other space when necessary, they are acting like friends. When two people are committed to each other, can fight and make up, and go on in their lives with greater knowledge and understanding of each other, they are friends. It is this ability to rely on another person and trust that he will be there for you that creates the foundation of any stable, loving relationship.

Plan Outings with Your Husband

What do you both like to do? Fish? Go antiquing? See movies? Before we became parents, we had all the free time in the world to have fun with our significant other. Once kids enter the scene, it can feel like free time evaporates into thin air. But it doesn't have to. One way to strengthen the friendship component of your relationship is by planning simple outings around your mutual interests. I emphasize "plan" because unless you set aside time and mark it on both your calendars, the outing may never happen.

2. Balance Your Roles: Partners vs. Parents

It's easy for parents today to get swept up in their children's lives. From the minute we take them home, put on their first diapers, and give them their first bottles, we begin trying our best to fulfill all of our children's needs and demands. While I am a firm believer in being a thoughtful, committed parent, I also know that if couples don't put their relationship first (most of the time), then no amount of devotion to their kids will keep their relationship alive.

That said, I also realize that it's not easy to keep a healthy balance between thinking of ourselves as both partners and as parents. How do we achieve the right balance that makes us feel that we are doing a good job as parents without losing sight of the reason you became a family in the first place?

Carve Out Time

Despite so many kids, so many demands, and so much enjoyment we get from our kids, Jim and I always carve out time for just the two of us. It's not always easy, but we don't waste time trying to figure out if we deserve it.

One night last summer we did just that. It was a Friday and I had been with the kids all week. I was exhausted and had spent all my energy reserves. As usual the kids had a swim meet and Jim and I had planned to meet there to watch them race. When he arrived from the office, we took one look at each other and knew we needed to create time for just the two of us. At the end of the swim meet, we took the kids to McDonald's (not something we regularly do) and then home. Once they were showered, in their pajamas, and set for bed, we headed out the door, leaving the older kids to babysit.

We didn't deliberate over whether the kids were okay—we knew they were safe and sound. And we also knew it was just as important for us to have time alone. We had a lovely—albeit short—dinner out and enjoyed every minute of it.

The best gift you can give your children is a loving relationship with your spouse. When children know—and witness—their parents putting aside time for each other, kids understand that their parents are committed to each other. They also know that their parents love each other. In turn this love between their parents makes kids feel safe, enabling them to grow unhindered, following their own unique destinies.

On the other hand when children are always put first or experience rancor between their parents, constant fighting, verbal violence, or a lack of trust, then children question the very root of their foundation. Such a lack of safety breeds internal chaos and insecurity—two obstacles to healthy self-esteem and confidence.

Show Your Love

For both your children's sake and your own, it's important to put energy into your primary relationship. Show your love toward him in front of your kids. Take time to be alone with your spouse. Your kids couldn't have a better gift than to know their parents love and respect each other and like to spend time with each other.

This also means that you have to save some attention for your man at the end of the day. When Jim gets home at night I will have his dinner place set with a pretty placemat, plate, and a big glass of water with lemon and sometimes a drink. I try to greet him at the door looking eager for him to get out of his car. I get off the phone so he knows I am focused on him. I will also kiss him. When he gets home, if I'm not right at the door, he seeks me out.

Taking Time to Reconnect

Even if you feel wiped out at the end of the day, you will feel reenergized simply by reconnecting with your spouse. Granted you may not have the energy to greet him with a beautiful smile on your face each night, but if you do it often enough, he will know that you care about him in that way.

Consider these ways to reconnect with your spouse:

- Plan a date night, which means putting a date on the calendar, hiring a babysitter, and making a reservation if necessary.
- Send the kids to their grandparents', friends', or cousins' house so that the two of you have a night alone at home.
- Talk to your kids about how important it is that parents have alone time. Explain that this doesn't mean they are

less important, but rather that a family's strength comes from the parents having a solid relationship.

- Hire a babysitter to take your kids out to a movie or mall and you and your husband can stay home alone—what a wonderful feeling to be alone. Have dinner uninterrupted! Your partnership is both an oasis and a source of strength, so give it the attention it deserves.

Ladies and Gentlemen

One way to ensure that you continue to think of yourselves as partners as well as parents is by treating each other with manners. If we as women treat our husbands like gentlemen, with courtesy, respect, and tenderness, they will be more likely to behave in the same way toward us, treating us like ladies. Letting him open a door for you and offer his hand as you get out of the car may seem like old-fashioned manners, but such simple gestures make us feel taken care of.

And a woman can take care of her man too by serving him dinner, doing his errands, or having the house look neat and tidy when he comes home. I am a bit old-fashioned, but I enjoy making my husband feel loved and cherished through my actions as well as my words.

3. Encourage Growth And Independence

In order for two people to say connected, they need to feel good when apart. And one of the primary ways you can assure this is by encouraging growth and independence in each other. Has your husband ever asked if he should take a business course to freshen up? Did you encourage him or did you ask him where he was going to find the time? Have you ever voiced a desire to learn a new hobby or return to school yourself and found your husband less than enthusiastic?

When I decided to get my personal training certificate, I knew the course would require a lot of studying and a big time commitment, which meant time away from my family. Jim was very supportive of my goal to become a personal trainer, and though it took some maneuvering of his schedule, he took over at home and even helped quiz me.

Recognizing Needs

He shows this same support for any endeavor I might have or if I need more emotional support. Sometimes he sits down with the kids and tells them I need more help around the house. Every so often, he will notice that I am not feeling well, too tired, and worn out. They all pitch in and help so I can have alone time to take a bath or go to bed early.

I'm not only talking about trying something new. One of Jim's passions is hunting with his father, brothers, and our older sons. He loves spending quality time in the outdoors, bonding among men. Although I am not that interested in hunting bear in the outback of Canada, I encourage him to take the time for the hobbies he likes, and I've even helped organize these trips when he doesn't have time to plan one.

Be Proactive

Jim also loves to work out with our older boys, and if I feel he isn't taking the time to do so, I encourage him to make the time. I've even been known to throw his workout clothes at him and say, "Don't come home until you work out!" It's very important that as partners we give each other permission—and encouragement—to do something we love without feeling guilty about it. I know (and Jim knows too) that he feels much better after a good workout. Sometimes I even join him!

The more positive we can be of each other's interests, encouraging each other to continue to grow intellectually, get in shape physically, or become emotionally healthy, the more we will feel supported in our endeavors. This support makes us as individuals feel empowered, independent, and self-confident. Such positive self-esteem is one of the primary building blocks of a healthy relationship.

Try Something New

Independence comes from confidence, and one of the ways to build confidence is to try something new. Regardless of whether we win or lose, succeed or fail, our belief in ourselves will grow when we put ourselves in a new situation and push our comfort level. What about trying something new yourself? Have you ever considered these activities?

Train for a running race. Whether or not you have ever run a race or even gone jogging, you might find enormous satisfaction in training for a road race. Many communities offer organized races throughout the year, especially in fall and spring. Check your local newspaper or library, where races are often posted. Then find a running partner who is also interested in training. After three months of walk-run-jogs you might be elated to discover just how far you can run, and how fast.

Learn to sew, stitch, or knit. Gone are the days when our grandmothers taught us such skills when we were kids. But it's not too late to learn. Many women find great solace and enjoyment from time spent sewing or knitting. They not only produce something tangible with their own hands, but they find it tremendously relaxing and satisfying.

Form a scrapbook club. Scrapbooking is a creative way to preserve your memories of your childhood, your relationship, and your family's history. Doing this with friends can add to your experience. Your friends can encourage you as you share your unique life story.

Join a book club. Reading a book and sharing your ideas with others who have read the same book is an invigorating, growing, and emotionally heartening experience. Over the years, the popularity of Oprah's televised book clubs has inspired thousands of women across the country to form their own formal or informal reading groups. Join one or form one in your neighborhood so you can discover the joy of reading!

Take a cooking class! This can be a fun and creative way to think about food, learn new recipes, and make new friends. Another way to learn new recipes and enjoy yourself with friends is through an organization called Time Out for Dinner. Once a month women get together to make multiple meals for their own families. For a fee, all the ingredients, supplies, and kitchen space are provided so that you can prepare dishes as a group (but for your individual families). The people who run the service post the menus each month, so you know ahead of time what dishes you will be preparing. The last time I went, I took home 12 meals to put in my freezer!

When we explore our world, teach ourselves new skills, and seek new experiences, we cannot help growing in confidence. We feel more satisfied with ourselves, more content, and more centered. It doesn't matter so much what you do but that you are doing something for yourself.

4. Build Trust

Trust is the glue of any healthy relationship because it is what a couple relies on to believe in their love, their bond with each other, and their future together. Quite simply, without trust, a relationship will crumble, from the inside out.

Yet trust is not instantaneous; it needs to be earned and it builds over time. When I was younger and first married, I had much less self-confidence than I do now. I was home alone with young children, feeling overwhelmed and unsure of my place in the world. Yes, I was a new mother, a young wife; on the surface I had my whole future to look forward to. But I hadn't yet developed the belief in myself that allowed me to trust in myself, in Jim, or in our relationship.

Self-Awareness

At times, I envied Jim's time outside the home when he went to work. When he would go out with his buddies, I wondered what he was doing and wished I had the freedom to be out in the world instead of stuck at home with the kids. At the time I couldn't see the importance of being at home with two young kids. Did Jim give me any reason to be suspicious? No. But because I was looking outward instead of inward for self-assurance, I was not paying attention to the reality that Jim was not giving me any reason—or evidence—to question him.

I didn't like myself acting or thinking in this way. Where had the spirited tomboy of my childhood gone? Where was the adventurous young woman who went off to Texas for college? As a new mother I had lost touch with myself. It was as if I hadn't yet integrated my old self (young woman) with my new self (young mom). When I became aware that I was both young woman and young mom, I also realized that I loved being a mother, I loved being married to Jim, and I knew in my heart that I had no reason to distrust my marriage. This self-awareness made me more at ease with myself, and as a result, my sense of emotional safety strengthened within my marriage.

Self-Confidence

More children were born. I watched our family grow. I watched Jim grow with our family, and I began to realize that I was growing too. The kids began to get involved in activities, and I was getting out more. I felt more freedom in my life, and as a result, I was becoming more at ease as a mother, more comfortable as a woman, and began seeking inner sources of my self-confidence. I grew closer to God and allowed His love to pour into my heart, into my life.

As I grew into myself, I began to realize something else about trust: that it is more about self-confidence than good behavior. When I feel content and comfortable in my own skin, trust in my relationship flows. But when I have moments of personal discomfort or I question myself, I can—without realizing it—project those feelings onto my relationship, second-guessing myself or Jim.

Of course, Jim has never given me one single reason to doubt him, question his actions, or wonder about his love for me, which is why now, 25 years into our relationship, the trust is there solid as a rock.

Weeding Out Seeds of Distrust

After speaking with so many women, I understand how seeds of distrust are planted and grow into enormous beanstalks, as if overnight. Some women who speak of a lack of trust in their relationships have good reason: Their spouses have betrayed them with an affair. Do you ever wonder why affairs are so crippling to relationships? Whatever the reason behind an affair, most couples cannot recover because an essential trust has been lost, fracturing the bond between the two people. Infidelity is an automatic trust breaker, and it makes trust extremely difficult to regain.

Yet other women, like me, who have never experienced infidelity also speak of trust as an issue in their relationship. Why? It usually boils down to a loss in self-esteem. As one woman I spoke to recalled, "Once my two kids were out of diapers and went to school every day, I couldn't figure out what to do with myself. I had worked before I got married, but I wasn't ready to return to a full-time job because I wanted to be home when my kids got back from school. I just moped around for about two months. Then I started obsessing about my husband—who was he having lunch with? Why wasn't he home by 6 p.m.? Did he stop anywhere after work? He was really confused by my sudden suspicions."

"Finally," she continued, "one night I just kind of lost it and broke down crying. Once I'd calmed down, my husband and I had a long talk. He suggested I get involved in some community service activities or join a fitness club. He was right. I really needed help getting my own life back. Once I made a few tiny changes, I felt so much better, and of course, all my jealous thoughts disappeared!" This woman is typical of many who become untrusting because they get separated from their own centers. The same can happen to men if they—for whatever reason—lose their grounding in life.

The next time you begin to hear jealous voices sounding in your head, ask yourself this question: "Is this about me or the relationship?" It's crucial that you keep the two separate, and yet it is easy to confuse the two. Remember the more aware you are of your own feelings, the more you can be objective about your relationship.

Do Something!

Is there something you can do in your own life, on your own time, to build your-self-confidence? You know there is! Just do it!

Do you make a conscious effort to treat your husband with loving kindness? This is not often easy in our stressful, busy lives. But being kind and loving is just as easy as being nasty and resentful—either can become a habit.

Do you speak to each other respectfully, without resentment, bitterness, or sarcasm? You can choose to speak to each other politely, kindly, and respectfully. When you do so, you connect to your love for each other.

Trust is based on honesty, integrity, and mutual respect—for each other and the relationship itself. It's about making our actions and intentions stem from our love for each other as partners and friends. Trust is what protects and insulates a marriage from danger—both inside and outside the relationship.

5. Show Pride

I'm not into flaunting my love for Jim in public, but I delight in giving him a compliment in front of others. I can watch his heart grow right before me. Openly expressing pride in each other shows that you admire your spouse and that you are not afraid to show it. While out to dinner with friends, it is very natural for me to brag about something Jim did that I was proud of. Recently I told some people what a great father he is and how much time he spends with our kids. As busy as he is, he always takes time to play sports and even coaches several teams each season. When I share this with our friends, Jim gets to hear my appreciation.

Be Specific with Praise

I don't hesitate to compliment Jim on how well he does with his business. When Jim gets positive reinforcement from me, he knows how grateful I am for all his hard work, which only increases his self-confidence. And he does the same for me. He loves telling perfect strangers how I do it all! He likes to brag about what a great cook I am and how I keep our house spotless.

We both make it a point to praise each other in front of the kids so they'll learn that showing admiration is a positive thing; they will also see again how much their parents care for each other. And the more children see and experience their parents' bond, the more healthy their experience of relationships will be. We also make it a point to speak nicely about our respective in-laws and families. Over the years I have heard so many people speak disparagingly of their in-laws, as if to prove the cliché true. When we choose to say loving things about our spouse's family, we simply increase the love quotient in our own relationship.

So next time you find yourself admiring your husband for a business or work-related success, looking handsome, or simply being a wonderful spouse, tell him. Your words carry weight only when spoken aloud.

If He Makes You Happy, Tell Him!

The longer two people know each other and live, work, and raise children side by side, the easier it becomes to forget to say things out loud. If he makes you happy, tell him! If you love the way he looks, tell him! The same goes for work situations. If Jim is feeling particularly good about a presentation or a business deal, I make sure to compliment him and tell him how I proud I am. It's important, too, to remind our husbands that we need acknowledgment for our work as well. Whether we work at home or in an office or on the road, we want our spouses to recognize our hard work and our accomplishments.

As one woman I spoke to said, "It *shouldn't* matter that my dishwasher is emptied by nine, the kids' rooms are clean by ten, and the rest of the house is tidy and organized by noon. But it *does* matter to me, and I want it to matter to my husband. So I ask him to please acknowledge things I do around the house. Sometimes I have to point things out. Did you notice I repainted the kids' rooms? Did you see that I got those photos framed and hung them in the family room? And when he tells me that he appreciates all that I do, I feel much better."

6. Pay Attention to Change

All transitions are trying and test the mettle of a couple's relationship. Indeed any change—large or small—can create stress and force people to adjust. These growing pains can be good for a relationship: They can force growth, strengthen resolve, tighten a bond. They are also rarely easy.

The birth of each of our babies has always been a time of joy and celebration. Yet the periods before, during, and after each birth always carried with them tremendous change and the need for readjustment. You would think we would have the process down pat, but that's not the case! From my first minute of morning sickness to the first contraction, we know we are in a nonstop period of change that impacts our entire family, but especially my relationship with Jim. I am more tired, and as the pregnancy develops, I can do less and less and Jim has to pick up the slack. He doesn't mind helping me out and doing more around the house and with the kids, but this extra work takes its toll.

Moving into High Gear

Once the baby is born, we enter that blissful yet challenging newborn phase when no one sleeps through the night. Babies require constant care and attention, which means Jim and I have less to give each other. Energy diminishes, patience wilts, and moods run ragged. This is when we go into high gear, making sure we are staying in touch with each other and sometimes giving each other more space.

Because change is stressful, it can breed distance between two people if they don't pay attention to their feelings and watch how they handle their reactions. Indeed, stress and distance between partners is often an indicator that some change is underway. Some changes are hard to miss because they are big and dramatic, such as a new job, a relocation, or a change in someone's health status.

Other changes are more subtle and don't necessarily send signals to us that change is afoot. The next time you feel unusually stressed or distant from your husband, consider what might be happening around you:

• Maybe you feel run down.
• Maybe a child is sick.
• Perhaps one of your kids is transitioning from one developmental stage to another.
• Maybe someone's feelings are hurt.

Dealing with Reactions

What changes have you gone through lately? Is it time to pay closer attention to each other? Make an effort to keep talking. If you have the sense that your spouse is bottling up feelings, then call him on it. If you're the one who's bottled up, open up. Ask questions. Give each other space. Be patient and extra kind.

Changes are hard but inevitable. It's how we react to them and deal with those reactions that can have the most impact on our relationships.

7. Keep Your History Alive

A relationship is not an enigma; it's a living, breathing organism with its own unique history. When the two of you actively keep your history together alive, you breathe life into your relationship, deepening your bond and paving the way for a strong, hopeful future. One way the two of you can nurture your friendship and relationship is by actively recalling the fun times you've had together, the sad times you have weathered, and the loving moments you will cherish forever. Thinking back on your relationship together helps you reconnect to those times that defined and cemented your future.

Relive Memories

Although Jim and I often relive our past, reminding each other of funny moments we've experienced together—from terrible decorating mistakes to a number of losing-things-in-the-trash stories—there are some special stories that capture the spirit of our marriage. One of my favorites to retell and relive is the time during my first pregnancy that Jim and I went out for Chinese food. I was eight months pregnant and very ready for baby number one to arrive. Since we hadn't yet been through the birthing experience, we were feeling both exhilarated and nervous.

During dinner I started feeling a terrible pain in my lower back. Without thinking I fell to the floor and (as Jim likes to remind me) began moving around in a crawl-like manner until I reached the center of the restaurant. (Our table was tucked into a quiet corner, so I managed to cover quite some distance in my effort to relieve the pain.) It was then that I began to vomit—in front of all the diners. The waiters became hysterical, running around and asking me frantically if I wanted hot tea. The people dining were aghast, and I'm sure a bit concerned, and Jim and I thought that I was beginning labor! When we got to the hospital, it turned out that I was not in labor (the baby didn't arrive for another two weeks) but that the baby had been pressing on my sciatic nerve—hence the pain.

For Jim and me this story captures our naivete as first-time parents—especially in light of the fact that we now have ten children! The image of me down on all fours, writhing on the floor of the crowded Chinese restaurant and vomiting amid the diners, is a bit disgusting but highly comical as well. There's something about that moment that brings us together in full force, making us experience our bond, our love, and all that we've been through, and ties us even tighter.

Cherish Memories

One couple shared a noteworthy first-date story with me. They were strolling around a small beach town. As they passed over a sewer drain, the woman's watch slipped off and fell down the drain. She stopped and said, "Oh, well. I lost my watch." Her date (and future husband) stood in awe of her response. "I would have been down on my hands and knees trying to recover the watch. It was so nice to see Sandy so blasé about material things. That's one of the things I now most love about her."

It can be wonderfully invigorating to recall the time you met or your first date—before you both knew each other well. Reliving your time together makes you cherish your memories and your future.

The Power of Respectful Communication

8. Keep Talking

One of the keys to remaining emotionally intimate with your husband is to stay in touch with how you both are feeling. Just because neither of you is complaining, don't assume everything is fine. If he's not talking, ask: Are you worried about finances? Is everything going all right at work? Do you feel more stressed than usual? Such simple questions can puncture a balloon of worry in an instant, as well as convey loud and clear that you care. Remember, there's more to life than worries, but it takes constant vigilance to keep the pressures of kids, money, and work at bay. And it's always a good idea to create time and space for just the two of you to tap into each other's lives.

With our busy household, it's easy for Jim and me to lose track of how the other is feeling, so we make it a point to check in with each other on a regular, almost daily basis. Ideally we like to put aside time in the evening before going to bed so we can catch up on each other's day, follow up on previous discussions, and just reconnect. But honestly, sometimes we are so tired that when we get into bed, we fall asleep as soon as our heads hit the pillows. Which means we need to carve out the time to touch base.

On weekends we first get the kids organized and busy so we

can have a few minutes of quiet. Sometimes we get up early or stay up late. We always find the time because we know how important it is to keep talking—it assures that we stay close and connected. Couples who divorce often say, "We just grew apart" or "We stopped talking." Take this as a powerful reminder to keep the lines of communication wide open!

Finding the right time to talk is challenging as well. If I am anxious to talk to Jim about something, it's never a good idea to broach a subject when the kids are running around or by blurting something out. I approach him gingerly. I gently touch his arm and ask, "So tell me, what's going on? I think we need to talk."

Communicating with each other requires delicacy, patience, and work. Yet the payoff is huge: Couples who learn to talk and listen to each other actively build support for intimacy.

9. Tone It Down

It's not just what you say to each other, it's how you say it. You might be angry, frustrated, and disappointed with each other—and for good reason—but a couple begins to eat away at the integrity of their relationship when they speak to each other in harsh, nasty, or sarcastic tones.

I know all about this because when I get frustrated or feel underappreciated, I sometimes strike out in a sarcastic tone. For instance, if I have prepared, cooked, and served dinner, and no one acknowledges my hard work or at least says that it tastes good, I am hurt. Sometimes instead of simply telling my family—especially Jim—that I would appreciate feedback when I cook dinner, I ask sharply, "How's dinner? Does anyone like it?" It's frustrating and hurtful when I've spent time and energy and they don't respond. On the other hand, when I become sarcastic, I only add to the bad feelings in the room.

On one particular morning we were all running late. The kids were getting ready for school, and a general sense of mayhem took over the house. Some of the kids asked frantically, "Are we having breakfast?" They are used to eating breakfast each morning and they didn't want to miss a meal because some of them were trying to gain weight for sports. Of course I was running behind, too, and hadn't yet put breakfast together. Then Jim said abruptly, "Are you going to make them some breakfast?" and I was really insulted by his tone. He made me feel like a short-order cook instead of his wife. But I felt even worse when the kids went to school without breakfast.

Later that day, when Jim came home, I said sarcastically, "Are you going to make them some breakfast?" He looked at me strangely and said, "What?" I glared at him—I knew immediately that he had no idea what I was talking about. All I had done was attack him and make myself look foolish.

Don't Let It Build

When I explained what was behind my remark, Jim apologized. But I had spent the entire day in a small fury and hurt his feelings on top of mine. If only I had said something at the time.

We are human. Our feelings get hurt. We get defensive. We strike back. But most of the time, resorting to a negative, attacking tone is not only unnecessary but also makes matters worse. You have to catch yourself before the words come tumbling out. Listen to the silent conversation in your head. "He's such a jerk. I can't believe he just did that" and so on. When feelings of anger or frustration start to build up, I try to take a break. I stop what I'm doing, I take a deep breath, and I take another minute or two to figure out exactly why I'm angry and/or hurt. (Nine times out of ten, hurt feelings lie behind anger.) When I take those steps, I am less likely to walk through the rest of the day mad. When I don't take those steps, I just make things harder for Jim—and me.

10. What Did You Say?

Everyone appreciates a good listener. And our husbands, above all, deserve our attention. When we are feeling frazzled and exhausted, what's some of the best medicine ever? To have someone listen to how we feel. We don't need that person to respond or offer solutions to our problems. We simply want to voice our troubles and have them received by a caring, thoughtful, attentive listener.

Talking Things Through

Jim and I do this all the time for each other. If Jim is getting ready for a business meeting, it helps him to organize his thoughts by talking through them out loud with me listening. And I am constantly asking him to listen to me as I process my thoughts and feelings. After our youngest was born, one of my best friends moved to another state. At the time, I couldn't deal with even thinking about her moving, never mind how I felt about it. Then when the baby was about two months old and things had begun to settle down at home, I turned to Jim and asked him to listen to me as it hit me how much I was really going to miss my friend.

When we offer—and receive—absolute attention from our spouses, we are strengthening the relationship's foundation of respect. Our willingness and genuine interest in hearing what the other has to say is a powerful way to communicate our love, our care, and our respect for that person.

11. Don't Nag

Whether you are a stay-at-home mom or a working mom, most women end up doing the lion's share of household work, errands, driving, and taking care of the kids. I know there are exceptions, and I honor the men out there who are stay-at-home dads, but for the most part, it seems women shoulder a larger part of the responsibility for managing the family on a day-to-day basis. They also resort to nagging when they feel their husbands are not doing their fair share of the work.

We all nag. It's hard not to. If you've spent the entire day straightening every room in your home, cleaning the kitchen after breakfast, lunch, and dinner, it can feel downright offensive when you have to pick up after your husband too. But shall I say it? Don't nag him. It's simply a poor reflection on you.

Breaking the Cycle
Nagging becomes a mode of communication for some couples. Instead of speaking directly to each other or addressing issues directly, they resort to indirect expressions of frustration that push each other's buttons and do more harm than good. Your car is a mess—why don't you clean it out? Can you ever do something to help me out? Don't you know where anything is in this house? The content is not important. It's the undercurrent of over-generalized complaint that is so hurtful and damaging. Why not say, "I

would really appreciate your taking the garbage out" instead of "You never take the garbage out!" One is a suggestion and request and the other is an accusation.

And though women are typically the part of the couple who nag, men are also responsible. It takes two to break the cycle. When I hear myself nag, I cringe. I hate the image of myself as a complaining victim. So I always try to catch myself. I try to turn my complaint into a suggestion, my accusation into a request. I have to admit, doing so takes energy and creativity, but a relationship without a nag is a relationship in which both people stand on equal footing.

12. Argue—The Right Way

Disagreements are par for the course in any marriage; if we agreed on everything, life would get dull fast. How many couples are there who never differ on any subject? And are they that harmonious in private? Just because couples fight doesn't mean they're doomed. In fact arguments can be a healthy way to process issues—if they don't turn nasty or degrading. It gets our blood pumping to fight every now and then, to learn how to argue and resolve our differences.

Vive la Difference!

I'll bet you and your husband fell in love in the first place because you balance each other out and you find your husband different enough to be interesting. Jim and I have been down this road. Though he appreciates that I am organized and on top of things, it's just that quality that used to bug him. I would remind him to do something or to bring home an important paper from the office. Of course I wanted it done immediately. Jim, who has enough on his plate at the office, would say, "Give me three days." I would push him and he would get angry—no big surprise—and we would end up in an argument. Over time we both became more cognizant of such arguments and learned to change some of our behaviors. In this case, I changed mine.

What I've learned to do when I need something from Jim is to give him enough notice so that he can work it into his schedule—not mine. As for the papers from his office, I simply retrieve them from his car myself!

One divorced woman I know told me that one of the primary reasons her first marriage failed is because she and her ex-husband never fought. "He's a psychiatrist, and it was important that we always talked things through. He would get very agitated when we argued or when I would raise my voice. I'm Irish—I have to raise my voice! Anyway, when I look back at that relationship, it's clear to me that if we were able to fight, argue, and get mad at each other, we probably would have let off a lot more steam. Our relationship may have even survived."

Letting Off Steam

It's crucial that couples express their feelings so they don't hold grudges or keep feelings pent up. There's no doubt about it: When we hold our feelings in, especially those that are negative, they grow and grow. After Jim and I argue, I wait until I'm calm and then I let him know of anything building up inside of me. I have learned to get things off my chest, not only with Jim but with everybody else too.

One thing my husband and I have done is talk about the way we argue. After we've had a disagreement, we often circle back at a later date and talk about what happened and what we said to each other. We discuss not so much the points we were making, but how we made them and how we reacted to each other. That way the next time we come upon a touchy subject or we have a fight, we know to focus on the delivery as much as the message. For instance, I like to be given a little time to come around instead of being expected to acquiesce immediately. And I will stand my ground if I feel strongly.

Giving each other the right to occasionally lose it (or become irrational) and then being strong enough to laugh about it later is wonderfully freeing. When Jim and I disagree, we always try to keep a few things in mind: Never be nasty; agree to disagree when necessary; and always make up in the end. Arguments are natural outlets for tension. When couples take this energy and learn to navigate and explore it, they can find themselves closer in a satisfying, fulfilling way.

13. Apologize and Forgive

The movie *Love Story* had it wrong: Love does mean having to say you're sorry. For a relationship to remain healthy, you have to be able to apologize and forgive all the time—even when it hurts your pride.

I remember one time when Jim and I had argued over how to discipline the kids. I tend to be more lenient, giving a few warnings before a consequence, and he tends to be more practical, giving maybe one warning before handing out a punishment. On one particular day, we had argued on the phone (he was at work and I was at home) over what to do with one of the kids, and things got heated and we both hung up on each other. I was so angry that I was unable to speak to him for the remainder of the day. The next day after he had gone to work, I sat down and wrote him a long letter, explaining why I disagreed with him, and I put the note on his desk for him to find when he got home.

It's Not Always Easy

As the day passed my thoughts about the incident became clearer. I realized that though I still believed I was right and he was wrong, I was uncomfortable with how I had behaved during the argument. By the end of the day, I removed the note from his desk, and when he came home, I apologized for my hurtful words.

Saying I'm sorry has always been harder for me than for Jim. To this day if he thinks he is wrong, he says he's sorry and that's that. He likes to get things off his chest. But I tend to stew and relive our fights. The older I get, however, and the more years we are married, I have begun to realize that I am just wasting energy by staying mad. The negative feelings drain me and become a burden to Jim, as well. So I now apologize. And though it's not always easy, I feel so much better afterward, like a burden has been lifted from my heart and our relationship. Knowing this—that I am freeing up both my heart and our relationship—is enough to make me the first one to apologize if we've had an argument.

Apologizing is not always easy. In fact, most of the time it requires a lot of strength and a willingness to put aside your pride. I find the push comes from my belief that our overall relationship is always more important than my temporarily hurt feelings. I trust that once I understand my own feelings, I will regret saying hurtful things or lashing out in anger. Therefore, I give myself time to process my feelings and always try to find the fortitude to say I'm sorry when I know I've hurt Jim's feelings.

Offering forgiveness is equally challenging but the process is the same: If we connect deeply to our love for our husbands (and they to their love for us), we are much more able to put aside a slight and move forward. Anytime I need to forgive Jim or he needs to forgive me, we connect to our love for each other. I have to trust that Jim never intends to hurt my feelings and he needs to trust that I would never want to hurt his. Then we are both free—free to forgive and let go.

14. Know When to Compromise

Most of us know we have to compromise, but we don't necessarily know how to do it. Or we think we are compromising when we really aren't. Why? Because attitude is more important than action. If the two of you are truly committed to each other and making your relationship work, you will be more likely to approach disagreements or conflicts with an open attitude—one that acknowledges that there are always at least two ways of doing things.

Jim and I compromise in a big way when the family travels. We are both efficient, organized travelers, and we both like to be in charge. But when we travel with our kids, Jim takes over. It's simply easier if there is only one leader. I may think I can handle things just as well as he, but in the spirit of compromise and peace, it makes more sense for me to step aside and let Jim be in charge.

Another example of compromise: After the birth of our youngest, I was walking to get back in shape. Instead of Jim doing his normal workout, he joined me on my walk. I know he would have preferred a more strenuous workout, but he went for a walk to make me happy and spend time with me.

Build Up to the Tough Issues

These may seem like easy examples, but easy examples give couples the practice they need to handle really tough issues.

If you and your husband get in the habit of compromising on movie choices, food selection, and routes to your destination, you will be more comfortable (and more likely) to develop a spirit of compromise. In turn, the ability to reach mutual agreements on tougher decisions, such as the purchase of a new home, car, or where to send your kids to school, won't feel so overwhelming.

15. Go Ahead, Help Him

There are many ways to show your love. What's important is that both people in a relationship realize that the other needs to hear that message. For example, Jim loves when I cook for him. I love to cook, and Jim enjoys good food. But more than that, he understands that when I cook a delicious meal for him or fix him a snack when he's hungry that what I'm actually doing is taking care of him. Food is a primary way that we can take care of the person we love. And on weekends I love it when Jim decides to barbecue or make breakfast. This is my time to relax and be served and his way of showing me that he loves me.

Different Needs

No matter how long two people have been together, and how well you know each other, it's still important to find out how he likes to feel your love. It's important to remember that the way he likes to be shown your love may differ from the way you like to be shown his love. Some couples experience a disconnect in this area. One woman I know always complains that her husband never buys her the right gift. When I asked her what he gives her, she said, "Jewelry." I know many women who would love to receive baubles from their husbands. But not this woman. She would rather he plan a trip away together. "I like doing things together. I want to spend time with him. We are always so busy with the kids and work; it's *time* that is most important to me."

How do you show your husband your love? Perhaps he likes to take walks with you or he likes watching movies together. Perhaps he appreciates your doing his errands for him or giving him a neck massage after a long day of work. Be sure to check in with each other: What do you need? What does he need? It's always better to ask than to assume.

16. Go to Bed in Harmony

You've heard this before: Don't go to bed mad. I'd like to put a positive spin on this cliché and stress the importance of harmony in a relationship. Most nights Jim and I fall into bed like tired soldiers. We are exhausted. Spent. But if we set aside even a minute for each other, saying good night and giving each other a tender kiss, we drift off to sleep with a tangible sense of our deep, loving connection.

On the other hand, when we go to bed mad, we can wake up disoriented and out of sync with each other. Knowing this, we try to make it a habit to be at peace with each other before bed whenever possible. Or course we don't succeed 100 percent of the time, but we strive for it. You, too, can make it your mission to forgive and let go before turning in for the night. By doing so you assure yourselves that the dawn will come in hope and love.

Keeping
the Romance Alive

17. A Little Lipstick
Goes a Long Way

It may sound old-fashioned, but I believe that just because women marry and bear children doesn't give us the right to let ourselves go. We may be tired or have no special reason to dress nicely or apply makeup, but once upon a time we were attractive young things . . . why let it all go to the dogs? And frankly, what husband wants to come home to a wife who looks as though she's been put through the wringer?

When a man comes home from work, what a joy to be greeted by a wife who seems fresh and lively, rather than beaten down. Of course, good men will continue to love their women despite those pesky extra pounds or a few new wrinkles—but it is the small, daily efforts we put into our looks that reflect our continued admiration and love for him.

Only a Few Seconds
Sure it takes time and money to look good, but it only takes seconds to put on some blush, comb our hair, and slip into jeans instead of stained sweatpants. It makes us feel so much better if we take a little care of ourselves. It's a way of

showing ourselves—and our husbands—some respect.

One simple way I like to make an extra effort is with my bedtime clothes. I'm tired at night like any mother, but I don't collapse into bed in a ratty T-shirt and stretched-out boxers. I put on a nice, bright cotton nightgown or pajamas that fit well and look cute. They serve as a reminder of the days when I had all the freedom and energy in the world. And I'm sure my husband appreciates the gesture.

During the day a touch of makeup or a pretty hairdo works wonders in making us feel like human beings. Let's avoid getting lazy about our appearances—it's actually easy to show ourselves a little respect, and we feel so much fresher and more positive as a result.

The same goes for how you greet each other at the end of the day. Why not meet him at the door with a smile? And remember, try not to start your first conversation of the evening with a complaint. That will surely get things off to a negative start.

Look Good—
For Him and You

Looking good means taking the time to take care of yourself. Here are some quick-and-easy ways I do it:

Get enough sleep. A good night's rest takes years off your face.

Give yourself a facial mask to perk up your skin.

Sit in a warm tub filled with lavender or other essential oils to refresh your body and mind.

Give yourself a pedicure and manicure—neat and trim nails work wonders on our state of mind.

Arch and trim your eyebrows with either a tweezer or wax.

Use a self-tanner to pick up your skin tone and your spirits—especially in the dead of winter.

18. Connect Physically with Your Man

It's the $64,000 question: How often should we be intimate with our long-term mate? Once a month? Once a week? Every day? We all have different notions of what "enough" is. I believe you have to show each other physical affection in the form of intimacy or cuddling, or simply a gentle touch in public frequently.

Lots of women feel that they have had enough demands on them: They are tuckered out from breastfeeding, comforting children, supporting spouses emotionally, or just plain picking up the house. Bedtime becomes a time to sink into bliss and rest their weary bones, not a time to rev themselves up and indulge in hours of physical intimacy with their husbands.

But it's not an all-or-nothing game. I think this trap can—and must—be avoided. Couples get lazy, especially the longer they're together. Sure we may not have lots of time, privacy, or energy, but this doesn't mean we can afford to lose our strong physical love for our partner. Your man must still be allowed to fill some of your physical and emotional needs, even after you have children.

Closeness

I like to think of it in terms of closeness, rather than sex. Ask yourself: Have I shown my husband that I need him? That he makes me feel whole and wonderful? You can do this in many ways, and one of the most powerful is physically. A kiss or a stroke of his hand when he says something sweet is often just the ticket. And the closer we are, the more natural it seems when we both fall into bed exhausted to reach for each other just to express our vital and deep connection.

No Kids in the Bed!

I love when my children snuggle with us in our bed—but there's a time and place for everything. In order for the two of us to remain partners first and parents second, we need to have our privacy, and so do you. As a rule, try not to let your kids sleep with you in your bed. Of course rules are meant to be broken—a sick child, a nightmare, a new baby. Our rule is "You can come to our room, but bring a blanket because you're sleeping on the floor." Still, many mornings we wake up with one or two—or more!—of our little ones tucked into bed beside us without our having known.

But sticking to the rule as much as possible will make sure that your private time with each other is protected.

19. Make Your Bedroom Your Sanctuary

It's easy for our homes to get overrun by toys, sports equipment, and other paraphernalia. And most of the time, I manage to keep clutter at bay and keep my house (mostly) organized and tidy. However, I make an extra effort to keep the bedroom I share with Jim special. I call it my sanctuary.

Our bedroom is always clean, with the bed made and pillows fluffed. I want the bed to look inviting and special. It has romantic, dim lighting, and I sometimes even light candles and sprinkle fresh-smelling powder on our sheets. As part of our commitment to each other, I feel it's important to respect the bedroom.

One of the main interruptions to intimacy is television. At our wedding a dear friend of the family gave us a toast and said, "Remember, no TV in the bedroom." After we had six or seven kids, he told Jim, "Maybe it's time to get a TV." If you can't bear the thought of removing the TV from your bedroom altogether, then try minimizing its usage.

Creating a Space

Creating space for the two of you to connect intimately takes a conscious effort, and rule number one is to keep clutter to a minimum. Consider these ideas:

- Put away clothes in the closet and dresser.
- Place knickknacks in a bedside drawer.

- Don't let newspapers and magazines pile up.
- Make your bed every day.

The bedroom you share is your special place, where it's all about the two of you. By keeping it tidy, you let nothing distract you from each other.

20. Date Nights Are a Must

Romance doesn't just happen; it has to be planned. This means you have to set time aside by working it into your week's schedule. When I want to spend a romantic evening with Jim, I plan ahead. I schedule a babysitter ahead of time, make a dinner reservation, and buy tickets or find out where music is playing. Then I e-mail him during the week and tease him just a bit about what I have planned. This is a great way to create the tension and anticipation that gets you both in the mood.

When we were in our twenties, it was easy to come up with romantic plans. But as we get older, we seem to do the "same old, same old" and later complain about being bored. Well, if you push yourselves just a bit, I'm sure you can figure out some fun things you can do even if you're not 20 anymore!

- Go dancing!
- Pick up take-out from your favorite restaurant and head to a nearby park for alfresco dining.
- Stay up late and watch a movie in bed (if you have a TV in your bedroom).
- Take a walk at sunset. If you live near water, so much the better. If not, find a park or a hilltop with a great view to the west, then make time to enjoy it together.
- Is there an old drive-in nearby? Grab a picnic dinner and cuddle in your car like teenagers.
- Go to a matinee on a rainy day.

There are plenty of ways to create a night of romance that don't require a lot of planning or money. If you can swing it financially, stay in a nearby hotel for a night. One couple I know does this every Valentine's Day. "It's kind of predictable and a bit cliché—but we really look forward to it. This year we were a little short on cash, so we went to a nearby motel—it wasn't glitzy, but we so enjoyed an uninterrupted night together!"

Date nights allow busy parents to get away from the responsibilities of home life and feel free and unencumbered. They also remind partners of their romantic connection, their physical attraction, and how it was they ended up being parents!

Romantic Movies To Watch Together

Make time for a romantic movie for two. Add your own favorites to this list!

An Affair to Remember
Breakfast at Tiffany's
Casablanca
Ghost
Love Story
Romeo and Juliet
Sleepless in Seattle
The Bridges of Madison County
The Princess Bride
The Thomas Crown Affair
Titanic
When Harry Met Sally

21. Stay Sexy in Your Mind

One of the hardest tasks for mothers in the trenches is to think of themselves as sexual beings. Amid poopy diapers, no showers until afternoon, and all the other distractions, how is it possible to retain that image of ourselves as a femme fatale that our husband fell in love with? To me feeling sexy is more often about how I feel than how I look. It's impossible to ignore the hundreds of daily images of perfect women's bodies that decorate covers of glossy magazines, TV, and tabloids. It's as if the world is saying that we are simply not sexy if we don't match Pamela Anderson's physique. But that is definitely not the case. Even nine months pregnant, I feel sexy. It's all a state of mind.

When my hair looks good and I put on something as simple as a new top, I can mentally transform myself from feeling like a tomboy mom to an attractive woman. But for me the single most important factor to feeling sexy is being in touch with my self-confidence. When I feel good about myself, when I've taken care of myself and made time to relax and restore my own energy sources, I feel at ease in my body and mind.

It's vital that women think of themselves as sexual beings. When they don't they risk losing a sense of their inner power. Cut off from this power, many women retreat and even withhold love and affection from their mates. And when they do, disaster looms for that relationship.

22. Stay Sexy in Your Body

One way we can stay sexy in our bodies is by taking care of them. Staying fit definitely makes me feel good about myself. I am getting older and have had several children, but I haven't let go of the need to feel physically strong and fit—it's a key part of my sensual vitality.

A woman I know who works from home takes her daughter to school and works out before starting her work. She doesn't shower until after her work is done. "It's my little ritual—for myself and my husband. I feel refreshed, I put on some makeup and perfume he likes, and I feel so much more desirable when he comes home. Thank goodness he doesn't see me all day!"

Create a Beauty Ritual

You don't have to be into fitness like me to stay sexy in your body. Another woman I know is sexually self-confident though she barely works out at all. Instead, what keeps her sexually vital is her beauty ritual. "When I want to connect with my husband, I know I have to get myself in the mood. I run a bath and put on soft music and light a candle. In the bath, I shave my legs, file and trim my fingernails and toenails, and wash my hair. This relaxes me and makes me feel good inside of my body. This is key to my feeling sensual and self-confident."

Our relationships depend on our feeling good about ourselves. You know yourself best. Take the time to make yourself feel good—mentally and physically—and you will experience a revitalized connection with your husband.

Get a Massage

One way to reconnect with your own body and make you feel sensual is by getting a massage. A massage does not have to be expensive. Many massage schools offer discounted services from students in training. Look for a massage school in your area and go for it!

23. Stay Connected When the Baby Arrives

The stress of caring for a newborn cannot be minimized, but it can be exacerbated if you don't stay connected to your spouse. During the first three months postpartum, most couples are so exhausted and their schedules are so crazy that the most loving thing they can do for one another is to be supportive. This may mean holding hands, snuggling in bed with your newborn between you, or simply giving each other some time away from the baby to do whatever—take a nap, a bath, or a walk in the fresh air.

The reality of postpartum is that women's hormones are going through dramatic changes on an almost daily basis. Women who nurse experience a very real slowing of their libido, as oxytocin, the so-called "nursing hormone," kicks in and takes over. Other women experience pain during intercourse after delivering vaginally. And women who deliver via cesarean section can take months for their bodies to fully heal. The bottom line is that it's important for each woman to honor her body and its natural healing time.

It has always been important to Jim and me that we reconnect intimately as soon as possible after the birth of a new baby. And I've been lucky. After all ten births of my children, four of which were vaginal, six of which were cesarean, my body rebounded without much pain or work. Because I did not nurse any of my children, my hormones regulated fairly quickly. The right time for a couple to resume their sexual relationship is a very personal, private decision, but I think it's important for both people to talk about it early on and to be aware of how the other feels. It's when the issue is treated silently, with neither person addressing it, that it can lead to problems later on.

24. Nurture Your Commitment

It's easy to assume that once married, you don't have to think about—or worry about—your commitment to each other. Nothing could be further from the truth. A relationship can thrive only if both parties continue to nurture their commitment forever. But how you choose to do this is a personal, often quirky thing. Many people take the symbolic route and celebrate anniversaries or give each other gifts such as rings to remind each other of their vows. Other couples take trips together so that, alone and away from home, they can reexperience the relationship they shared before the kids came along.

Jim and I nurture our commitment in several ways, but one particular event stands out from the rest. We truly enjoyed the time we went on a spiritual retreat. Jim had wanted to travel to a sunny destination together for our anniversary, but a priest friend suggested to Jim that we celebrate by going on a retreat and we both loved the idea. Over the weekend we reconnected spiritually, learned more about ourselves as both individuals and as a couple, and listened to how other couples related. We also prayed together. The whole experience brought us closer together, deepening our bond.

How you celebrate your relationship and find ways to nurture your commitment to each other is up to you; the bigger point is to remember to do it.

Treating Each Other In a Special Way

25. Accept Each Other

In many relationships, women try to improve on their men: influencing their habits, encouraging or discouraging certain interests, and even insisting on living a preferred lifestyle. We're wired this way! But once you've been together for a while, you know each other's imperfections, annoying habits, and ways of doing things, and it becomes a waste of energy to try to change each other. I think it's more productive and less self-righteous simply to accept each other.

Perhaps after a long, tiring day your husband likes to zone out in front of the TV and you like to read; perhaps he prefers to wait until the end of the month to pay bills, but you like to pay them as they come in; perhaps he takes a quick, 5-minute shower, but you like to luxuriate for fifteen. No two people are exactly alike, no matter how much they love each other or how well they get along. We will always do some things differently from our spouses.

Respect Differences
One friend of mine says she always makes the bed in the morning as soon as she and her husband wake up. She used to complain about it to her husband. "Why don't you ever make the bed? Why do I always have to make it?" Then one

day she realized that her husband did other things that she never did, like take out the trash—a chore she abhors! She certainly didn't want her husband harping on her to start dragging the trash cans to the end of the driveway on Tuesday mornings in the middle of winter! So now she simply makes the bed without another thought.

I've known and loved my husband for more than a quarter century now, and there are plenty of ways we do things differently. I tend to make quick decisions and Jim is more thorough and pays more attention to detail. I like to stay up late and talk; Jim would rather get up early and get things done. Like the friend I mentioned, I have come to realize that complaining doesn't get me anywhere and only makes me feel bad.

There's reciprocity in kindness and acceptance. If you open your heart to a positive approach to your husband's way of doing things, you'll find he'll do the same when confronted with your way of doing things. And you'll be grateful for his patience. In the end, it's a win-win and everyone benefits.

26. Review Your Values

Jim and I are lucky. One of the most enriching ways we connect is through our shared values. To us, these values cement our relationship. We both believe in the importance of faith, family, and community. We treat each other with trust, honesty, and respect.

And we try to act on these values as much as possible. For instance, we make it a point to eat dinner together, show respect for elders, and behave in a loving, respectful manner toward our parents.

When life gets busy and we are running in several different directions at once, it's easy to lose sight of these values. That's why we make it a point to remind each other of them. For Jim and me this outlet lies in prayer. Praying together enables us to quietly yet deeply commune with God, who brings us together. In such special times, we ask for grace and stay in touch with the values that tie us and our wonderful family together.

27. Keep Materialism in Check

As Americans we are blessed with abundance, a positive thing unless we get caught up in our possessions and the desire for them. Regardless of how much money people have, it's easy for couples to get caught in a cycle of always needing more or the next best thing—whether that's a bigger house, a better car, more toys, clothes, or CDs! Indeed in our society it's acceptable to try to "keep up with the Joneses." But this attachment to material things can keep two people on the outside of their relationship, caught in things superficial, rather than connected on the inside at the level of the soul.

Sometimes couples need to keep check on each other. I have some women friends who get caught up in ordering tons of clothes and furnishings from catalogs. They don't need half of what they order and they also have trouble paying for it. Do they tell their husbands about this silent-but-deadly obsession? No. The end result? One person is hiding something from the other, which can lead to mistrust and dishonesty.

Breeding Disaster

Here is a profound story of how materialism almost destroyed a couple. Married for almost 40 years, Barbara and Mike looked like the picture-perfect couple. They were always dressed to the nines, were warm and charming, regular churchgoers. All three of their adult children were happily married with successful careers. Suddenly one of the daughters received a distressing call from her mother, saying that Mike had become seriously ill. What was behind the illness? Barbara soon discovered that not only had Mike put them into colossal debt, owing many banks and credit card companies hundreds of thousands of dollars, but that he had been borrowing for years. Barbara felt like their whole life had been a sham. The expensive home in the well-to-do neighborhood. The Louis XVI furniture. The jewelry he had given her over the years. None of it was paid for. Once Mike recovered from surgery, Barbara tenderly confronted him. What did he say? "I did it all for you. I wanted to make you happy."

Though not divorced, Barbara and Mike now live in an unhappy state of mental seperation, unable to trust each other, comfort each other, or love each other.

This story may seem like an exaggeration. Sadly, it's true. And it's also not that uncommon. Materialism can breed disharmony, distance, and disaster.

28. Be Realistic

Once we grow up, we quickly realize that real life is not like in the movies. We grew up dreaming of love, romance, freedom, money. We didn't think much about mortgages, health issues, boredom, or difficult decisions. Becoming an adult, a wife, and a mother means our lives are brimming with wonderful experiences, and tough ones too.

In my opinion, approaching adult life with the understanding that it can't always be smooth sailing helps a person tackle the hard times with a can-do attitude. Your feelings toward your husband and marriage are bound to dip and surge; this is just real life. Sometimes you'll feel close and in sync, other times you'll argue like wildcats . . . or wonder what on earth attracted you to him in the first place. Thinking long-term—that we're in it for the long haul—is the key to moving toward better days. Every phase passes eventually, so don't make life harder by getting mired in the present.

A Higher Purpose

When faced with a family crisis (whether it has to do with health, behavior, or circumstances), I tackle it knowing that ahead of me lie moments of intense happiness and joy . . . if only I can get there. And I'm lucky; I surf the waves of life supported by a loving family. But even if you struggle without family help, know two things: You are never alone, and for every dip in the wave there is a crest right behind it.

My belief in God helps me accept that I am here on earth not only for my own satisfaction but for the betterment of mankind. It sounds lofty, but I believe that every experience, great or small, positive or negative, helps me become a stronger and more worthy person.

29. Find Meaning Beyond You

One of the most important ways that Jim and I connect and give meaning to our marriage is through our mutual commitment to service. When we help others, we infuse our relationship with purpose beyond ourselves. And we do this constantly, in whatever ways we can. We reach out to our sisters and brothers and their children. We offer to help our parents. We contribute to our church. We donate clothing, food, and money to people in need.

I tell you this not to burden you with yet another obligation or to toot my own horn, rather because I have found that the more Jim and I have connected to our community and to lives outside of our own, the more we have strengthened and bolstered our own relationship.

Giving Back

A powerful example of this commitment to others occurred a few years ago when Jim and I watched Oprah's African AIDS television special. It aired about a month before Christmas, around the time I typically get overwhelmed by all the pressure this holiday brings.

As we watched Oprah talk to the children and observed glimpses of their poverty-stricken lives, Jim and I were truly moved. The stark differences between us and them put Christmas into perspective for us. Together we decided that

that Christmas our focus was not going to be on amassing toys and gifts for our children but on spending time with each other and our kids. We also decided to give to kids in need by donating to Oprah's benefit, as well as to local kids' organizations. The result? We experienced one of the most joyous and relaxed, peaceful holidays in years. Jim and I felt united and at peace—with each other and the rest of our family.

Going beyond our own lives and giving to others—in whatever way—helps keep the big picture in perspective. This perspective bars against selfishness and invites communion. Couples who enrich their lives through such acts of selflessness gain meaning and purpose in universal proportions.

30. Reach for Joy

Every day can be a source or inspiration for joy. To me joy is the miraculous ability to experience true happiness. It's an awareness of life's beauty. It's an engagement in the splendor that's all around us. And when you experience any of this with your husband, you take your bond to a whole new level—one that is deeper, more spiritual, and closer to God.

How do you reach for joy? By laughing together, praying together, going to church together, experiencing nature together, or listening to music together. The avenue varies and it's entirely up to you as a couple—but the goal is to let the world slide away and for the two of you to come together, two souls as one.

Of course the births of each of our babies have been moments of ecstatic joy. We feel this kind of joy each time we witness an accomplishment or honor that our kids have received. But we also feel this joy each morning when one or more of our children comes into our bed. As I wake and see their faces, my heart leaps. When we pray together at night, my soul reaches for Jim's. He and I together thank God for all our blessings.

Your Family & Kids

In this chapter

This section was written to help you with your own questions about children and family. Read the whole section, or, as with the other two sections, use this mini table of contents so you can find what you want quickly.

Your Family & Kids

As mothers nothing motivates us more than our instinctive drive to keep our children safe and make them happy. We want them to have fun, but we also want them to be happy, to learn how to make confident decisions, to become responsible, and to find fulfillment along the way. On top of all of that, we want them to be respectful and mannerly! Needless to say, these illustrious goals, while possible, are not at all easy to achieve.

Raising children can be draining and stressful, but it's also a pursuit that's filled with laughter and joy. Some days are more difficult than others, and I find myself throwing my arms in the air and dreaming of retiring to a deserted island. But I know that without my kids, I would be nowhere: nowhere near the happiness and joy they bring me again and again; nowhere near their loving, smiling faces; nowhere near their hearts which grow right before my eyes each and every day.

All About Attitude

I was a teacher before I was a mother, so I learned a lot about how to achieve a balance between rules and chaos, worry and neglect, underinvolvement and overinvolvement. What worked best in the classroom was finding a productive middle ground between the extremes where I could feel comfortable being flexible, showing concern, and being involved. I have found this middle ground as a parent too.

I feel that we get from parenting what we put into it: If you want to inspire joy and laughter, you will find joy and laughter. If you focus only on the stress and challenges, then that is what will pervade your vision. In many ways, it comes down to attitude. As a mother, I seek a balance between casual and thoughtful. I try to be casual enough to remain flexible so all ten of my miracles are free to grow in their own unique ways. I try to be thoughtful so they learn about themselves and their world in a safe, reasonable way.

Managing Your Family

I hope the following essays help you in your quest to raise happy, healthy, confident children who can become the best they can be and give something back while they're at it. Some of the essays are inspirational and are meant to encourage you as a parent and to instill emotional skills and spiritual wisdom in your children so they become kind, thoughtful, and compassionate. Other essays focus on how to help your kids navigate the world around them: school, organized sports, homework, and the daily onslaught of the media (from television to films to the Internet and computer games). I also share tips on how to teach kids manners so they respect people (including their parents!), how best to discipline behavior, and how you can effectively teach your kids to eat well, sleep well, and exercise so they learn how to take care of their bodies. You'll also find information to help you better navigate school systems, determine the right balance between under and overinvolvement in your child's school life, and find the best pediatrician for your family.

I'm one of those moms who definitely errs on the side of overorganized. It's in my nature to find a place for everything and everything in its place—a good thing when you have ten kids! With that in mind I have included lots of tips on teaching your kids to become organized, better time managers, and how to take care of their belongings. But even if you are not super-organized, you can incorporate strategies that will help your home run more smoothly, your kids get more organized, and your life become much less stressful. Who isn't interested in being less stressed?

Role Models

What I've come to realize and understand over the last eighteen years of child rearing is that while parents can do a lot to raise educated, thoughtful, and well-adjusted children, we cannot do everything nor should we. The best parents can do is to offer their children love, a safe home, guidance, faith, and opportunities to learn about themselves and the world they live in. They can also provide good examples for their children by being role models of both behavior and attitude. As I told Oprah over three years ago, it is my dream to raise self-confident, respectful, responsible human beings who can give back to the world.

"The best parents can do is to offer their children love, a safe home, guidance, faith, and the opportunities to learn about themselves and the world they live in."

Your Child's Heart
1. Kid for the Day

All children need to know they are inherently special—not just because they are beautiful, smart, athletic, funny, or well-behaved. They need to know they are special without any conditions attached. And yet in our busy lives, it's difficult for us parents to remember this simple but powerful truth.

My typical days begin by making everyone a big breakfast. Afterward I'm out the door by 8 a.m. and driving from school to activity back at school to home to more after-school activities, almost without pause. Under this kind of time

Birthday Celebrations

We love to celebrate birthdays at our house! The birthday girl or boy is definitely Kid for the Day, but he or she gets feted in other ways too. Sometimes I take a baby photo, blow it up, and laminate it into a placemat. I place photos of the birthday boy or girl at different ages on the table, surrounded by presents. I also play the video of the day they were born. The kids love this tradition! The birthday kid wears the birthday hat and hangs the birthday flag on the house. Then at mealtimes, we go around the table and each member of the family describes why he or she loves that person.

pressure, and with so many kids getting in and out of the car throughout the span of the day, I rely on a simple game I call "Kid for the Day" to remind me to treat one of the children to some extra attention that day. Whoever is Kid for the Day gets to sit in the front seat of the car on the way to and from school. He or she also gets to pick which radio station we'll listen to in the car. As a finale, the Kid for the Day is exempt from kitchen duty before and after dinner that evening.

The kids love this game and look forward to their special days—even my older kids appreciate the gesture and being able to communicate in a more one-on-one way. When a child is sitting next to me in the front seat, I am able to ask direct questions, make eye contact, and really get a sense of how his or her day went or is going. I get to tap into the heart and mind of that particular child, letting that child know how unique and loved he is.

In the best of all possible worlds, we would all like to spend special time with each of our children—whether we have one, two, or ten, like me. But it's a difficult task to accomplish. Kid for the Day makes doing so more plausible but cannot do the job completely. It's up to parents to make sure each child feels special by accepting who that child is—regardless of his or her personality or temperament.

2. We're in This Together

A child's first sense of belonging comes from his or her understanding that he or she is part of a family unit in good times and bad. Regardless of how that family is defined—one parent or two, single or divorced parents, stepparents or adopted parents, one sibling or none—a child needs to know, and be supported in knowing, that she belongs to an entity larger than herself and that her place in that family is meaningful.

Jim and I remind our kids of the importance of family by encouraging them to adopt an attitude of "we're in this together." We want them to feel like we're all connected to one another whether we are together or not. For instance, it's virtually impossible for both Jim and me to attend all of our children's games and activities. Time conflicts and work conflicts and other miscellaneous conflicts sometimes prevent us from being there. But when Jim or I cannot make a child's game or activity, we send the siblings to support that person in the game. All the kids know that wherever they are, they are together.

Expect Kids to Pitch In

If situations arise in which disagreements or fights occur, our kids know that we expect them to stick up for their siblings and to help one another.

The "we're in this together" attitude also means working as a family in the home. All our kids are expected to pitch in around the house, take responsibility for their chores, clean up after themselves, and offer to help one another (or their parents!)—without having to be asked. Living side by side means kids have to learn how to cooperate and how to be respectful of privacy and personal space. It means they learn to respect others, and they avoid becoming so self-absorbed that they are unable to empathize when someone feels down or troubled.

Defending Each Other

On one occasion one of our sons misbehaved at the dinner table. When he didn't respond to a couple of warnings, we asked him to leave the table and to sit in the corner to collect himself. One of his older brothers disputed both the crime and the punishment and asked to speak on behalf of his brother. He argued that the inappropriate hand gesture of his brother was not an example of bad behavior (our viewpoint) but simply a matter of relieving an itch. After hearing this, Jim came up with the idea to do a mock trial. Trying not to laugh, we watched as the two brothers presented a trial with witnesses, a judge, and a jury consisting of the remaining siblings.

While Jim and I may not have been entirely convinced of our younger son's innocence, we were duly impressed with the brotherly demonstration of "we're in this together." And, of course the misbehaved son got out of his punishment!

Our kids are not perfect, far from it. They fight and argue like all kids. But they understand that no matter their differences, they still have to live under one roof, a feat which requires mutual respect, support, and cooperation. When kids learn this attitude at home, they are better equipped to go out in the world feeling confident in their ability to get along with others, work with others, and enjoy others. My kids have learned to value belonging and understand why the family connection is something never to be taken for granted.

Here are some suggestions for fostering a "we're in this together" attitude in your home:

- Remind your kids that they are part of a family.
- Teach your kids about their responsibility for honoring their connection to that family.
- Praise them for protecting one another.
- Acknowledge fights between siblings and encourage them to work things out on their own, with your supervision.
- Treat everyone equally.
- Don't compare siblings.

3. Tell Stories and Reminisce

Have you noticed how much kids love to hear stories, especially when they involve their own flesh and blood? Your life and your family's past are treasure troves of fascinating stories to pass on to your children and beyond.

Jim and I love telling the kids about their heritage: sharing stories of when we were children and when their grandparents and great-grandparents were young. We also encourage them to ask their grandparents to tell stories of when Jim and I were young. They can be any kind of story: silly and fun ones that illustrate the humanity of their loved ones, difficult stories that teach them that some issues stay the same even in different eras, and stories that show how their loved ones surmounted obstacles, just as they will in their own lives.

Lessons in Stories

The beauty of these spoken tales is that the detail and context I give them can change according to how old the kids are and what kind of behavior or experience I'm trying to model for them. One of my favorites is when I was nine years old and I finally could pull enough hair back to make a ponytail like my older sister. I was so proud of my new ponytail that I left it in when I went to bed. In the middle of the night my dad came into my room to check on me because I had been crying in my sleep. Earlier that evening he had been harping on the fact that I shouldn't do anything without a light on, like read, for example. So I dutifully had turned out the lights. When he patted me on the head to comfort me, he thought the lump in my hair was gum. Never turning on the light, he got scissors and cut out the gum. It wasn't until he went back to his well-lit room that he realized what was in his hand—my new ponytail!

My kids love that story—it brings their mom to life at an age they can relate to. They enjoy both the humor and my understandable disappointment when I awoke in the morning to see my hair shorn!

One of Jim's favorite stories happened when he was 6 years old. He and his older brother were outside playing and his brother told him to climb the neighbor's swing set. The neighbor's German shepherd (which Jim was scared to death of) was tied up. Once Jim got to the top of the swing set, the boy who lived in the house directed his dog to attack Jim. The dog chased Jim, so he ran back to his house and jumped through an open window, which was four feet off the ground. The kids love to imagine their ever-so-strong "Pop" running in fear for his life!

Oral Traditions

Sometimes I tell family stories instead of reading to the children at bedtime. Oral traditions give them a rich sense of family on which to build their self-esteem. I also show them old pictures around which I create a story—sometimes these stories are real, sometimes imagined. Either way the kids love to imagine and follow along. (We have framed photos of our

Reading Aloud Never Gets Old

Reading aloud helps kids get into reading. It is a wonderful way to spend time with kids, especially on long car trips. Make sure to take turns for older kids to read aloud too. Here are some of my favorite books for different age groups:

For Ages 2–5
Curious George series, *Corduroy* books, *The Giving Tree, The Pokey Little Puppy*

For Ages 6–9
I Spy books, *The Boxcar Children, The Baby-Sitters Club series*

For Ages 10–12
Chicken Soup for the Kids' Soul, Old Yeller, Charlotte's Web, White Fang, The Call of the Wild.

For Ages 13–15
The Catcher in the Rye, The Adventures of Huckleberry Finn, Let the Circle Be Unbroken

For Ages 16+
As I Lay Dying, Hamlet, The Kite Runner, Catch-22

parents, grandparents, and great-grandparents hung on a basement wall where all the kids can look at them—they love to discover family resemblances with their relatives!)

Most people love to reminisce—encourage your parents and family members to do the same. You can create a picture book of new and old family photos with your child or write a piece of fiction using a family member as a character. Or help them base a story on some family lore, altering it slightly to heighten the drama.

Family stories are also a tender way to remember loved ones who have passed away. By talking about them, they live on in your child's imagination. I like to focus on positive memories without dwelling on death or hardship. And children who appreciate the circle of life understand that memories live on throughout the ages; they are less fearful of their own mortality. The varied experiences of our families are jewels in the rough just waiting for us to bring them into the light so they can dazzle.

4. Enrich Their Lives With Rituals and Traditions

Rituals and traditions bring a family together by emphasizing the bonds that make you a family. For us, holidays are rich with traditions, and our Christmas abounds with several diverse rituals.

Create Your Own Rituals and Traditions

A ritual or tradition is any activity that you repeat in a way that has meaning for you and your family. Although many of our traditions coincide with holidays, a tradition can happen at any time of the year. What does your family enjoy doing together? Here are some ideas:

• Go camping, take a hike, or visit a national park. The outdoors is a wonderful venue for families to spend quality time together and to bond more deeply.

• Take a ride to visit the resting places of deceased relatives. Reminding children of their relatives, even those who are deceased, heightens their sense of family relationships and helps mitigate any negative associations with death.

• Let the kids prepare a meal for the grown-ups! Children love to play in the kitchen, and teaching them cooking skills and giving them the responsibility to prepare a meal enriches everyone's appreciation for dinner!

One of the first things we do in preparation for Christmas is set up a beautiful manger, awaiting the birth of the baby Jesus. For every good deed, a child may add a piece of straw to the manger. For every bad deed, the child must remove a piece of straw. The goal is that by Christmas, Jesus will have a soft, comfortable manger made from acts of love and kindness.

In addition to the living room's formal Christmas tree, the kids decorate their own tree in the family room. On it, they place whatever decorations they love or have made throughout the years. One year we had a few hockey sticks jutting out from the top, tennis rackets balanced precariously among the branches, and ballet slippers dangling delicately from the garland. Picture frames made of Popsicle sticks and other handmade ornaments abound. This is their tree after all, and they trim it with whatever they like!

After Christmas we take all the Christmas cards and place them in the center of the table in a basket and pray for the families throughout the year at our family dinners. If we receive 100 Christmas cards, then for the next 100 days after Christmas we are praying for someone. This is a special ritual that keeps the spirit of Christmas alive beyond the holiday itself and also reinforces the presence of others beyond our walls.

At Easter we relive the Passion. The kids do a play, we watch religious movies, turn the TV and radio off on Good Friday, and restrict older kids from going out from Holy Thursday to Easter.

Our family also celebrates the holidays with traditional foods. At Christmas, my mother makes a delicious Greek soup called avgolemeno (egg and lemon soup) and Jim's mom makes a delicious Boston brown bread.

Rituals

Although these rituals are very much tied to my family's religious faith, there are many ways for families to adopt their own traditions and rituals regardless of religion. Birthdays, Father's Day, Mother's Day, graduations, or other special occasions present good opportunities. One family I know climbs Mt. Washington every spring in honor of their grandmother who grew up nearby and climbed it each spring. This family of three children looks forward to their special spring event with the greatest of anticipation and delight.

Several years ago, we began celebrating an annual "Tardy Party," which came about during a spell of time in which the kids were always running late in the morning and, as a result, would be tardy for school. As an incentive to get to school on time, Jim came up with the idea to have a party to celebrate those who avoided being late to school. The kids would be able to invite whomever they wanted and it would truly be their party. Now it's an annual event—with Jim presiding over fifty or so boys and me taking care of the girls at home (a smaller number of course). They design and make T-shirts for the occasion and have a blast!

5. Give Them Your Attention

Paying attention is one of the most powerful ways you can show your children you love them. I always try to smile whenever one of my children walks into the room. I make eye contact, give them a hug or a kiss, or make some other gesture to show them I love them. In response my kids are always excited and joyful to see me. The younger ones run toward me with arms out, and the older kids make it a point to find me to say hello and good-bye.

When kids know you are paying attention, it's as if their hearts grow larger, their brains stronger, and their bodies more durable. So next time your little one wants you to watch her go down the slide, watch her. Or attend a ballet recital, attend. Or listen to a reading of a poem or class report, please listen.

Show Your Children You Love Them

We love to tell our kids we love them, and we do so often. But there are many ways to show your kids your love for them. We call the kids nicknames related to their successes. If one of the kids scored three goals during a game, he'll say, "What's up 3-Goals?" Here are some other suggestions for making sure you get your message across:

- Say "I love you" before they go to bed.
- Hug or kiss them as they head off to school in the morning.
- Give your child a nickname or pet name.
- Say "I love you" on the phone before hanging up.
- And don't forget Kid for the Day (on p.181)!

6. Show Up

I know as well as any parent that it's not possible to make it to every single game, performance, or practice. But you can show up at their activities, sports, or performances some of the time. And you can show an interest in their lives, ask them about school, their friends, and their feelings more often.

I absolutely live for going to my kids' games, shows, and recitals. Not only does my being there make that particular person feel special, it also reinforces and supports our kids' hard work and practice, encouraging them to continue in the future. When we remember, Jim and I bring the video camera or camera when it is a big game. When we show up, the kids always spot us immediately and wave from the field or stage.

Showing up means just that: You are there for your children as their most passionate advocate, their cheerleader, their most loving supporter in life. Your presence is testament to this love and they will carry it inside themselves from this day forward.

When You Can't Be There

We all feel guilty when we're unable to attend our kids' activities. On most days kids understand that if you can't come it does not mean you don't want to come. I remember one day pulling up at one of my kid's baseball games and signaling for him from the car. From centerfield, he looked at me with a giant question on his face. I motioned for him to come and then yelled, "Come on! We have to go to another game!" He looked at his coach, shrugged his shoulders, and ran off the field! Nowadays this is less likely to happen, but when all the kids were younger, many of the games started at the same time or overlapped—I didn't have much choice! But it's still difficult for us to watch all of their games—the lengths of the games alone make it fairly impossible.

When conflicts arise that get in the way of your being able to attend an activity or accompany a child to a function, try some of these tips:

• Call your kids at least once during the day. A simple check-in call, in which you ask about school, friends, or other activities, can mean the world to your child. This kind of gesture also helps your child feel connected to you throughout the day, not just when you walk in the door after a busy day.

• Have someone videotape the event so you can watch it with your child when you return home.

• If you can attend part, but not all, of an event, do it. Sometimes moms think that it's a question of all or nothing. But not to a child. Being there part of the time is better than being there none of the time.

• Send someone—an older sibling, an aunt, a favorite caregiver—in your stead. When neither Jim nor I can attend a game or presentation, we send one of the older siblings to attend. That way the child playing or performing can look into the audience and see someone from the family, even if it's not mom or pop!

7. Be an Emotional Coach

Kids don't automatically understand how they feel or know how to articulate their feelings. Especially when they are young, kids need help identifying their feelings, putting names to those feelings, and learning how to manage the intensity of feelings, especially negative ones.

Is it hard being around a child in a bad mood? Yes. Sometimes we want to shake the moody child and say, "Snap out of it!" But we can't. Can you imagine if someone did that to you? Yelled at *you* for feeling sad? Criticized you for feeling afraid? It's best to respond to your child's unpleasant mood with love.

A parent must be an emotional coach on a daily basis. Here's what I do to help my kids deal with their feelings and emotional entanglements.

Different Stages

Little ones—Small children get moody, and it's usually because they are overtired, haven't eaten, or feel overstimulated and need some peace and quiet. Most of the time, they will feel much better after a good night's sleep (or nap), a healthy snack or meal, or some downtime. However, if one of my younger kids wakes up in bad mood, I will say, "You and I will have a lot of problems today if you are in a bad mood, so let's be friends and have a nice day. Plus, it makes me sad when you are mad. I love it when you smile." It's important to teach young children early about their feelings so they can begin to identify how they feel and communicate that to you, their parent.

Older kids—Adolescence brings along more complicated emotional situations that kids need to process and take care of. Getting along with their peers at school has suddenly become much more complicated than it was in elementary school! I pay close attention to any shift in moods at this age and make sure I ask a lot of questions about whom they hang out with at school, how they are feeling, and if anyone or anything is giving them any trouble. Since I don't want to solve their problems for them, I guide them through situations by role-playing. For instance, when one of the kids is asked to spend the night by a friend but he or she doesn't want to go, I help by suggesting ways he or she can tell his/her friend without hurting the other person's feelings. This way our kids learn they can't simply avoid the situation (not call the friend back) but instead need to address it.

Coping Skills

Children experience complicated emotions, and though we can't alleviate all their turmoil, we can try to help them understand their feelings and give them skills to cope with their emotions. Here is some general advice:

• Make it a point to know what has happened in your child's life that precipitated or caused a specific feeling or change in mood.

• If your child is too young to articulate or recount an event, ask his or her teacher what happened. Do some

Create an Oasis Every Day

Kids are busy with school, activities, sports, and homework, so no matter their age, they need downtime. For this reason, I build an oasis into each and every day by giving my kids a time and place to relax. Often this time occurs after their homework is done and before we sit down for dinner. If the day has gone according to plan, I will have already finished preparing dinner ahead of time so that this window is my time to just hang out with the kids doing nothing.

investigating. You can find out information if you keep asking until you get to the bottom of the situation.

- Make your questions as specific as possible. For example: "What happened at school during lunch today? Who did you play with? Was anything different at school today?" Think of yourself as part mother, part detective.

- Help your kids identify their feelings. With younger kids, you need to play more of a guiding role by suggesting explanations or words that capture how they feel. For example, if you think your child is sad, you might say, "Are you feeling sad today? Are you disappointed that Johnny didn't want to play with you at school?" Older kids need less guidance and more room. You want them to feel comfortable confiding in you. They may not share the reason behind the feeling, but they may share the feeling itself.

- Support and empathize. Don't try to talk a child out of feeling a particular way. Instead let him or her know you understand how he or she feels and that feelings will pass; they always do.

Peer Pressure

We all know that peer pressure can be brutal and messy. There's no avoiding it, but parents can help their kids prepare for it by giving them some tools to manage it:

- Encourage your kids to form their own opinions.

- Explain that they may encounter pressure to be like other kids—in behavior, dress, or opinions.

- Discuss ways they can remove themselves from situations where they are uncomfortable so that they have a plan ahead of time.

8. Write Love Letters to Your Children

Love letters aren't just for grownups. Kids love nothing better than to be surprised by a good, old-fashioned love letter from their parents. One of my friend's strongest memories from her childhood was finding a homemade, heart-shaped card in her packed lunch on Valentine's Day. To this day she can't remember who sent it, but she still treasures the memory. Why? The written word is powerful.

A few years ago Jim and I began writing special notes to each of the kids and putting the notes in their desks at school. We'd include a piece of candy or some money, and the kids were flabbergasted when they found these special missives. Now other parents are doing the same!

Letters are a thoughtful, tangible, lasting way to say what you mean. If you're away from your kids a lot for work or pleasure, they'll love knowing that they're still in your thoughts. You can hide love notes under their pillows or in their sock drawers when you travel. Here's one I left for my three-year-old when Jim and I went away for a long weekend:

Dear Carmen,

We have the photo of you being born with us in our suitcase so that when we miss you, we can take it out and look at your smiling face.

We love you and we will see you on Sunday!

Love, Mom and Pop

In your note, you can tell your kids where you are going, for how long, and also how much you'll think of them and miss them.

I also love to include messages of confidence in my missives, such as "I know you'll do well on your math test on Tuesday" or "Good luck in your soccer game next Thursday." Being specific lets them know that I care about the details and know what is happening in their lives on a day-to-day basis. There's nothing like knowing your busy mom thinks of you as a priority to bolster your self-esteem. When we give children concrete evidence that we know what they are doing while we are away, and that they are always in our thoughts, they feel deeply and permanently connected to us, and they walk taller for it.

Love notes are good for the parents who write them as well. I feel less guilty and more in tune with my little ones during times when I just can't be there for them. I'm happy when I know my children feel treasured.

A Joyful Home

9. Clarify and Communicate House Rules

Regardless of how you and your husband decide to run your household, the most important factor for kids is that you communicate the rules and expectations clearly. In our house, everyone shares in the responsibilities of household chores, including changing the water bottle, putting away empty milk bottles, replacing toilet paper and soap, making beds, taking out the trash, and keeping personal items in designated lockers. Kids are not allowed to talk on the phone after 10 p.m. or take a soda without asking. One of our most important house rules is that whatever is discussed in our house stays in our house. Another is that our house rules still apply even at someone else's house. These house rules help make our home run smoothly, reduce chaos and clutter, and teach our kids how to be responsible. We also have regular family meetings during which we gather around a table and tell one another what is bugging us about the other. These meetings are cathartic but not always easy. It can be painful to hear negative things about oneself, but in the end, these meetings release tension and clear the air. For this reason, we always end the family meeting on a positive note and our family feels closer than ever.

Parents are the most important factor when it comes to clarifying, communicating, and reinforcing the house rules. Here are some tips for parents:

- Decide on what you want rules for (sweets/dessert, sleeping/bedtime, nights out, TV, computer).
- Discuss the rules themselves and agree on how to approach situations in which rules are broken.
- Communicate these rules to your kids and describe behavior expectations clearly, repeating the rules whenever necessary, especially for younger kids.
- Be consistent but also be flexible: There are always cases when the rules can be suspended.
- Follow through on consequences for not following or abiding by the rules.

How parents choose to discipline those who break rules is a personal and private decision. In our house if our kids disregard the rules or misbehave, they get at least two warnings about

Say No Creatively

There are creative ways to say no without saying so. Instead of constantly saying "no" to your children, try beginning, "Yes, you may, but after you clean your room" or "Yes, you may go out tonight but only if you've finished your homework." By being creative, you can save the declarative "no" for the important, no-negotiation situations.

changing their behavior or they will be grounded or lose a certain privilege such as talking on the phone or watching television. For younger kids, the lost privilege is usually a play date or a sports game. Older kids are grounded from going out with their friends. If after two warnings (I sometimes give them more) the behavior persists, then the offender is absolutely grounded. No matter how painful—to them or us—Jim and I stick to our guns.

Computer and TV Rules

Our rules for TV and computer use are fairly straightforward. We don't allow computers in bedrooms. All the computers in the house are in public areas and are monitored by parental controls. And we don't allow instant messaging on the computer. The televisions also have locks so the kids can watch only age-appropriate shows. TV viewing is limited to a certain hour, depending on age. As a rule Jim and/or I try to watch TV with the kids—this way we can always see what's on and television watching becomes more of a family-oriented experience.

Reining in Toddlers

It's always hard when our bubbly little babies begin to make the transition into toddlers. They bite, pinch, cry. As babies we don't pay the behavior any mind. But as the child rounds the corner from one to two years old, we are presented with a child who needs boundaries and limits. "No!" is our least favorite but most often used response to toddlers. There's no doubt that toddlers need boundaries and limits—for their own safety and to begin to learn how to behave. But keep in mind, until kids are about two years of age, your "no" can be confusing. Developmentally, toddlers are programmed to explore their world, and the word "no" is an abstraction they cannot understand. Here are two strategies to use in addition to saying no:

• Redirect their attention by getting them engaged in another activity. This way kids don't get caught in a temper tantrum when they don't fully understand why you are saying no.

• Show how to do something through your actions, not your words. Kids are visual, especially little ones. If they see you doing something, they can then mimic the behavior.

10. Make Mealtimes Joyful

How often do you stand, dazed and confused, in front of an empty fridge? Ever make dinner with ancient leftovers your kids can't even recognize? Sometimes making food for kids can be a real bore. It's hard to be imaginative and diversified, it's hard to find time to shop well, and often it's hardest of all to get kids to eat without complaining!

But food is sustenance for the soul, and dinnertime offers a great opportunity to spend time with your children, eating and talking. Meals can make for joyful occasions, and here's how I do it.

Plan Ahead

On Sunday nights I think about the meals for the week, often asking the kids what they'd like to eat and even sending older kids to get the foods they want. I also browse through cookbooks and sometimes bring them with me when I shop.

On Monday I then do a big shop. This way I have a plan for meals for most nights and don't have to spend my week worrying about when I can get to the grocery store with a car full of kids in tow.

By organizing meals for the week ahead of time, I save myself a lot of aggravation. I write a list of the dishes my children love, those they'll tolerate, and the ones I want them to eat. I include everything I can think of (this comes in handy for babysitters too). Then I devise a simple plan for each week that includes one or two meals from each category.

By planning ahead we can begin to think of family meals as a time to slow down, focus, talk about our day, and pay attention to each other in a way we rarely do when we are up and about, involved in myriad everyday activities. If you go crazy trying to come up with ideas for nutritious, easy meals, ask a few friends for the meals they make the most often: You'll be surprised by the variation and it will liven up your own repertoire. Every now and then, I rotate a cereal night or a breakfast-as-dinner into the routine—the children love it!

Weekends are special, so let yourself off the hook: Allowing a little leeway for spontaneity makes life a lot more fun. I also put the kids in charge and have them make their own pizza or suggest they eat breakfast foods—that they can prepare themselves—for dinner!

Quick Recipes That Work

Breakfast:

I am a big believer in breakfast. Here are four great breakfast meals my kids love:

- Scrambled eggs with cottage or cheddar cheese
- Breakfast steak on a bagel
- Salsiccia and eggs, scrambled or fried
- Bagels with melted farmer's cheese on top

QUICK RECIPES:

Breakfast steaks: Take thin slices of steak (or pork loin cutlets); fry with olive oil or grill; top with seasoned salt and pepper.

Salsiccia: Salsiccia is Italian sausage made of chicken or turkey, found in Italian groceries or specialty stores. Grill or cook the salsiccia in a pan with olive oil; squirt lemon freely.

Dinner:

Dinner is one of the biggest meals of the day. Here are some of my kids' favorites:

- Breaded turkey cutlets with potatoes and broccoli
- Pasta (penne or rigatoni) with my meat sauce (or a three-meat sauce) and lemon-oil salad
- Greek salad

QUICK RECIPES:

Turkey cutlets: Take thinly sliced veal scaloppine; dip in egg or olive oil and then cover with seasoned bread crumbs and grated Parmesan cheese; add to hot skillet; squirt with lemon.

My meat sauce: Mix crumbled lean ground beef with 2 large cans tomatoes, 2 cans tomato sauce, 1 small can of tomato paste, ½ cup sugar, 2 bay leaves, 1½ teaspoon salt, pepper, ¼ teaspoon red pepper, 1 teaspoon Jane's Crazy Mixed Up salt, 1 teaspoon fresh parsley, fresh basil, garlic, onion, and olive oil to taste; add grated Romano cheese. For the three-meat sauce, add cooked ground pork tenderloin and salsiccia to the meat sauce for added flavor and richness.

Lemon-oil salad: Mix green lettuce (Boston, Bibb, romaine, and iceberg), and mint; then add cherry tomatoes, kosher salt, and cracked pepper. Dress with 3 tablespoons of either fresh squeezed lemons or lemon juice and add 1 tablespoon olive oil.

Greek salad: Salad is made of raddichio, Boston or Bibb lettuce, sliced tomatoes, red onion, feta cheese, pitted kalamata olives; dress with red wine vinegar, olive oil, and ½ teaspoon sugar.

Dessert:

Who could forget dessert? Two favorites are my apple pie and chocolate chip cookies.

QUICK RECIPES:

Apple Pie: The crust is made with 2 cups of flour, 1 cup shortening (I use Crisco), ½ teaspoon salt and slowly add ½ cup of cold water. Refrigerate overnight in wax paper. Then slice 6 or 7 Golden Delicious apples, add 1 cup sugar, 2 tablespoons flour, a dash of cinnamon, nutmeg, and salt. Put 2 tablespoons of margarine on top of filling before laying crust over it. Pinch ends of crust and fork-hole it. Bake at 400 degrees for 45 minutes. I use a 9" Pyrex pie pan.

Cha-Cha Chocolate Chip Cookies: Mix 2¼ cup flour, 1 teaspoon baking soda, 1 teaspoon salt, 2 sticks lightly salted butter, ¾ cup sugar, ¾ golden brown sugar, 1 teaspoon vanilla, 2 large eggs, 24 ounces semisweet chocolate chips, 12-ounce white chocolate chips. Mix until blended and then freeze the batter overnight. Bake from frozen at 375 degrees for 9-11 minutes.

11. Mind Their Manners

Kids learn manners from their parents, and they don't learn them overnight. Teaching our kids manners means modeling the behaviors ourselves. It takes focus and lots of repetition. So if you're in the process of teaching your kids table manners, social niceties, and other ways to show respect, be prepared to repeat yourself—again and again and again. I receive compliments on my children from other parents and adults all the time; and hearing this praise about how well-behaved and polite my kids are means the world to me.

We make a conscious effort to sit down for family dinners at least four nights out of seven, working sports schedules and other activities around dinner. Sitting down as a family is important not only for following through on manners but more important for staying in touch with our kids and what's going on in their lives.

Teaching by Showing

Family dinners are opportunities to show our kids how to eat in a mannerly way, how to hold a fork, use a knife, not to slurp from a spoon, and to sit up straight and not slouch. We point out how to ask for something to be passed, where to keep their hands (in their laps unless they are eating), where to put their elbows (not on the table), and how to use their napkins. The kids who are old enough help set the table, prepare dinner, serve and clear, as well as clean up. Family dinners are lively, loud, and filled with laughter and are an important centerpiece to our family life.

In the same vein, you'll need to clearly explain how you want your kids to introduce themselves and meet people. We make sure our kids look a person in the eye, shake hands firmly, and say, "Nice to meet you." Don't assume kids understand how and when to make such verbal gestures. You'll also need to remind them to say "Hello" and "Good-bye"! Eventually they will get the hang of it.

We show our kids how to answer the phone when someone calls by saying, "Hello, Sansone residence." We also teach them how to call someone else's house. They say, "Hello, Mrs. Smith. This is So-and-So Sansone. May I speak to So-and-So, please?"

Teaching your children good manners is a gift you will give them for the rest of their lives. They will carry themselves better, treat others with respect and politeness, and all of their good behavior and comportment will be a wonderful reflection on you as parents.

Manners for Restaurants

Your kids learn manners at home, but they are more likely to use them when dining out. It's important that parents teach kids how to behave in a restaurant.

Here is some advice:

- Keep voices down.

- Don't get up and down; stay in your seat.

- Address servers with "Yes, ma'am" and "No, sir" and always be sure to say please and thank you.

- Insist kids dress up to go out to eat so they know this is special.

12. The Magic Message Board and Events Calendar

There is a limit to what you can keep in your head. With all the notices from school, the changes in soccer schedules, the plays and recitals and volunteer duties, the driving and fetching and watching, there is no earthly way you can keep it all straight without approaching it like a Marine. The secret to keeping track and staying sane: Write things down!

I use an 18x24-inch whiteboard (you can use any size that suits your needs; also, these can be found at most crafts stores) that erases easily so the kids and I can write down any important appointments or reminders on a daily basis. It hangs next to the phone and my main calendar. Everyone can check in with it to see who has practice, games, and doctor's appointments. You can leave phone numbers on it for the babysitter, reminders to yourself, phone message notes, or even a daily to-do list.

It's all about having a specific location for information that is accessible to all; believe me, it will bring well-earned peace to your household.

Kids love these boards; they like being in the know. They can write down what they need or remind you of something important. And when they're old enough to answer the phone, they can write down the message for you instead of promptly forgetting it. I encourage my kids to use the board thoughtfully, and I hope to instill in them good organizational skills.

The whiteboard can serve as a source of inspiration as well as instruction. I like to head it with a positive phrase for the day, such as "Practice Makes Perfect." It's a great way to make life easier and teach important lessons at the same time. I also put up Happy Birthday messages and let the kids know where I am and when I will return.

Keeping a Calendar

My calendar is positioned next to the whiteboard. As soon as I get schedules for my kids' practices, games, rehearsals, or information from school, I write them down on a master calendar that relates exclusively to kid activities. I also transfer everything that goes on this master calendar to my own pocketbook-size organizer (as simple or complex as you like) so I can check my availability on the fly. That way when a friend asks about a play date, or I'm at the salon trying to set up my next hair appointment, I won't risk overbooking.

Every Sunday night I check my calendar to see what's in store for the next week. I also use this time to e-mail the week's schedule to my husband so he knows what's going on. During the week, I check my calendar daily as I drink my morning coffee. Once the calendar is created, I can send copies to grandparents and other friends. This system will help you to figure out in advance when you'll attend an event, and you'll avoid being a flake and not showing up because you've forgotten or booked something else.

13. Create Family Time Each Day

To us, family time is precious. It's time set aside exclusively for the twelve of us to acknowledge how grateful we are to be together and to have such a wonderful, loving family. Since we are a family in continuous motion, we have to make a concerted commitment to create this family time so that it will happen.

As I mentioned earlier, we try to sit down as a family for dinner together at least four times each week. Our meals together are a vital part of our family time since often we are all going in different directions. If we haven't had family time at dinner because of sports practice or games, activities schedules, or homework commitments, then we make it a point to gather as a family before going to bed for the night. We will use this time to talk about our days or we play games. This is when we will have a family meeting, sharing grievances or hurt feelings.

Count Your Blessings Together

We gather often as a family to pray. By praying together, we let the kids know that we are all one family and that God loves each and every one of us. We thank God for all His blessings and express our gratitude for our health, happiness, and safety. This time together makes the kids feel secure and strengthens their faith that there is a God who is loving and caring for them.

Granted some nights such gatherings are impossible, given all the kids' schedules, practices, and varying bed times (remember, I have several kids under age 6!). But we try, and often enough, we make it happen.

14. Create a Safe Home

When our kids are infants and toddlers it's easy to remember to safeguard electrical sockets, windows, doorknobs, stairs, and cupboards that contain dangerous chemicals. But even when the kids are grown, we must watch out for their safety. Accidents happen all the time, and many end in tragedy. It is always better to be safe than sorry.

Remember to:

- Install smoke detectors
- Install window latches or safety windows
- Keep a fire extinguisher handy
- Cover electrical sockets
- Test annually for radon or carbon monoxide

Have kids:

- Use seat belts
- Wear bike helmets
- Wear ski helmets
- Take swim lessons

Never:

- Leave a child unattended in the bath
- Leave children unattended near a swimming pool

Skills for Getting Along in the Real World

15. Nurture Confidence and Self-Esteem

We can all dredge up images from our memory banks of not fitting in with the kids at school, the pain of losing a friend, or the difficulty in just feeling good about ourselves. Just as we did when we were growing up, our kids are going to confront challenges to their self-esteem.

But what is self-esteem? To me, it's one of those words we all throw around and use loosely without really understanding clearly what it means. When I observe my kids struggling with their homework, practicing their sport, or even trying a new food at the dinner table, I see confidence at work. Each and every time a child steps outside his or her comfort zone and tries something new, he or she is allowing his or her confidence to grow. As a result, his or her self-esteem will grow as well. When we as parents help nurture our children's inner support system, that child has the opportunity to grow and flourish.

Bolster Self-Esteem

One of the key ways that we as parents can help our children develop positive self-esteem is by giving them opportunities to grow and learn and by accepting them for who they are. As a teacher, I always dressed my bulletin boards with a big pair of reflective sunglasses and a note that said, "Here's looking at you!" It was my mission to let kids know they are valued for who they are, not for who someone else wants them to be. As a mom, I continue to focus on this. Recently one of my kids was getting discouraged and frustrated with his schoolwork, and I saw his confidence begin to slip. It wasn't enough for me to help him anymore, so we hired a tutor (we paid). He did a 360-degree turn for the better, and everyone noticed—they were all so impressed that they wanted to hire the same tutor for themselves!

Another child failed several spelling tests. I had him buddy up with one of his siblings and asked them to work together, side by side. The challenged speller is now receiving perfect scores. He is standing much taller too because he feels so proud of himself. And an added bonus is the special bond created between the two siblings.

Even with their children's best interests in mind, parents can sometimes make matters worse. By excessively praising their children, giving too many pep talks, and overprotecting or rescuing their children, parents can devalue a child's self-esteem.

Self-esteem builds over time, and parents, as much as children, need to be patient, as well as encouraging.

Checklist for Growing Self-Esteem

❏ Know your child.

❏ Accept your child for who he or she is.

❏ Give your children opportunities for success.

❏ Be patient and realistic with their developmental stage and skills.

❏ Don't limit your child by categorizing him or her as a certain type of person.

❏ Don't compare one child to another.

❏ Remind your children that they can accomplish their goals, but they will have to work for them.

❏ Offer praise for specific, measurable successes.

16. Give Your Children A Moral Compass

Jim and I feel strongly that one of the most important parenting tasks is to give our children a moral compass and teach them values that will guide their actions and behaviors now and forever. We focus on instilling values such as honesty, respect, kindness, compassion, forgiveness, and charity.

How do we accomplish this?

• Be thankful for what you have.

• Remember the less fortunate.

• Get kids involved in service projects, such as taking them with you to deliver food or clothing to the poor.

• Organize and throw a party for kids at a group home.

• Donate or buy holiday gifts for families in need.

Walk the Walk

This starts with you, first by actions. Parents need to walk the walk, not talk the talk. In our house, we clean out closets at least once a year. Each child brings down what he or she doesn't wear or what no longer fits and offers these clothes to the next youngest child. Whatever the next child doesn't want, goes to the less fortunate. One year, one of my sons tried on a "cool" pair of pants handed down from his brother. They fit and he loved them, but he said, "Why can't we give these to the poor? Why give only what we don't like?" So we gave the cool pants to the poor.

I used to take the kids to orphanages, and we would throw a party for them with cake and ice cream and our kids served them. We also brought new toys and clothes. My kids wanted to see the children they were helping, and now my kids remember these moments with great fondness. I know they will continue to be aware of and be generous with the poor throughout their lives.

The best way to ensure that your children grow to become kind and compassionate adults is to teach them how to be kind and compassionate children.

17. Teach Kids How to Succeed—and Fail

Children are under tremendous pressure to succeed, and parents feel tremendous pressure to help them succeed. But what does success mean? Going to the right school? Getting straight A's in all subjects? Winning an athletic scholarship? Sure, those are laudable goals, but they may not necessarily mean your child will be happy or feel successful. To me, success means helping our children understand who they are, giving them opportunities to discover what interests them, and guiding and supporting their attempts to use their gifts to their fullest potential.

That said, parents need to keep in mind that all children are different. They come into this world with their own unique personality, temperament, skills, and interests. Parents must help each individual child find his or her own interests.

We can also help our kids become self-reliant by helping them to learn to make decisions for themselves. Heaven knows, we are not going to be around to do things for them forever. Self-reliance is the umbrella that enables children to know themselves, accept themselves (i.e., their strengths and weaknesses), and develop the confidence to make the best possible choices for themselves. Learning to make sound decisions means giving your kids the opportunity to try new things, allowing them some freedom to make their own choices, and helping them accept and learn from their mistakes.

Teaching kids to be self-reliant also involves helping them learn to accept life's inevitable losses as well as wins. When our kids win or succeed we always give them a hearty congratulations and let them know how proud we are of them. And while we praise their performance, we also make sure they know we are really proud of them for trying so hard and winning. When they don't succeed, we do the very same thing: We give them a big hug and a warm congratulations and we let them know that we value them, their hard work, and their great sportsmanship. We look for them to do their best—win or lose—and use the gifts God gave them to their fullest potential.

Share Your Own Losses

One of the best ways we can teach our kids the value of success and failure is by sharing our own successes and failures. When my kids lose an important game or do poorly on a test, I recall the story of when I lost in an important tennis match. After getting into the finals of a championship, my doubles partner and I lost. Was I disappointed, my kids want to know? Of course. But it didn't stop me from continuing to enjoy tennis and play in matches.

Kids need to know that failing—or not winning—is part of playing the game. We all lose some and win some. Kids need to become comfortable with both the idea and the reality that practice is necessary, that we are not perfect, and that there is always another chance to get another, perhaps better, result.

Balance Praise
with Constructive Criticism

It's important to praise our kids for things well done, but it's just as important to offer constructive criticism when appropriate. Start by pointing out something positive, then tell them how they can improve another aspect. That way they'll be more likely to listen (and benefit).

18. Give Value to Work and Money

With so many extracurricular activities and commitments, fewer kids have the opportunity to work after school or even during the summer. For this reason, parents need to make an extra effort to teach their kids the value of both work and money. Kids should grow up understanding what their parents do to earn money (work!) for their household and how they can learn to earn it as well. Making this connection early on will help foster a respect for work and money.

My father taught me lessons about hard work and money early on. His father died suddenly when he was just sixteen. As the oldest son, my father became a major financial contributor to his family. When it came time for him to go to college, he earned a football scholarship to cover his tuition, took classes at night, and worked during the day so he could continue to support his family. This early experience helped to shape the man and father my dad was soon to become.

Work Before Play

When my sisters and I were young, our father woke us up on summer mornings with a hearty, "This is not Camp Locho!" Everyday he reminded us very early in the morning that we had our chores to do before we would be set free to run wild with the rest of the neighborhood kids. There we'd be: mowing the lawn, picking up trash, cleaning out the garage, and doing other chores until our father finally released us! And most embarrassing was instead of wearing our sneakers with our shorts and t-shirts, we had to wear awkward, hard shoes to protect our feet while lawn mowing. Did I complain? I'm sure I did. But I know now that this respect for work, which translated into respect for money, made me appreciate the value of a dollar.

Nine Dollars

As a mother, I try to instill the same values in my kids. One time I had six or seven of the kids in the car. I had just picked everyone up from school and they were all hungry, so I pulled into a Subway and said, "Here's nine dollars."

My oldest son said, "What are we going to do with nine dollars?"

"Get what you want and then bring me a Diet Coke." I replied.

So they all filed into the Subway in their school uniforms and I went to get gas. When I returned, they came running out and handed me a Diet Coke in a cup with wet soda drippings down the side. I said, "You did it?"

"Yes," my oldest son nodded. "We split a couple of 6-inch subs and some chips and bought one cup. Then we all stood in front of the fountain. I had Dr. Pepper and then handed the cup to her. Then she had her soda and handed the cup down to him, and so on. When we saw you pull up, we filled it with Diet Coke." He was smiling, clearly proud of what they had accomplished as a team and with nine dollars. And hence my cup with drippings.

Kids learn best about money when they are challenged to do so. Parents can encourage respect and value for work and money by:

- Talking to your kids about jobs you and your husband have had.
- Letting your kids know what you do for a living.
- Explaining what work means to you.
- Linking the idea of work to earning money and lifestyle.
- Taking your kids to work for a day.
- Setting up a bank account and encouraging them to contribute any cash they earn or receive as gifts into the account.

19. Teach Kids to Manage Time

If kids learn how to keep track of time, become efficient, and well organized, they will take these skills into adulthood, becoming productive, accomplished adults. Like so many things, these skills have to be learned over time, and parents need to be patient and resilient in their encouragement and support. I know this firsthand.

Every Wednesday my first-grade son brought home a story for me to help him read. He forgot his story one week, and the next week, I asked him to get the story out of his backpack. As he rummaged through his backpack, out came papers from two months prior, permission slips I never saw nor signed, empty Frito bags, and so on. He was nervous and his face got red when he realized he'd forgotten again. He looked up and said, "Look at the bright side. I have no homework." I kissed him.

So what did I do after kissing my disorganized first-grader? I helped him by reminding him each day to do his homework immediately after school, empty his backpack of papers, organize his homework assignments for the week ahead, and continuing to reassure him that he can and will succeed at being organized.

Prepare Ahead

When kids learn how to prepare ahead of time—whether through practicing for a sports event, doing homework, studying for a test, or laying out their clothes the night before—they get into the habit of thinking ahead. Refer them to the message board and the daily calendar so they can see what's on their schedule for the week. If they are too young and not reading yet, then it's up to you to tell them what's happening ahead of time. You may be the one to gather their things beforehand, but you are laying the groundwork for a lifetime of thinking ahead and being prepared. It's never too early to teach them this valuable lesson! Remember, kids learn by example and by rote. If you show them the way, they will learn. But some more than others may be naturally more efficient—so be patient . . . and kind!

20. Organize Their Physical Space

One way to reduce clutter in your home while teaching kids to mind their belongings at the same time is to compartmentalize their things. In our house, I have created several areas for the kids to neatly place their backpacks, clothing, jackets, sports equipment, shoes and sneakers, and other belongings.

• **Cubbies**—Each child has his own cubby with his picture in it. They keep backpacks, coats, shoes, belts, and any other personal items they need on a daily basis.

• **Mud Room**—This area is right by the door that leads outside where the cubbies are located. I also put the seasonal sports baskets in there. In the fall, the baskets are used for soccer and football uniforms; in winter, they're used for basketball; in spring, they're used for baseball equipment and swimsuits.

• **Storage for equipment**—I use trash cans for hockey sticks, hats, etc. I put up inexpensive plastic shelving for cleats, Rollerblades, helmets, etc.; and use big crates on wheels for all balls.

• **Kids' rooms**—They have closet space for most clothing, dressers for underwear and socks, a desk (a farm table with a drawer makes for two desk areas), and two swivel chairs. A big closet for junk.

• **Attic**—I use the attic space for all Christmas items.

• **Garage**—My garage is like a store. If a child needs something new for a sport, he or she heads to the garage before going to buy something new. There is shelving on walls for helmets, football equipment, cleats, water jugs, hockey bags, lockers with locks for hunting gear, and hooks for hanging bikes from the ceiling.

Organizing takes time and effort, but once you have created a place for everything, everything will have its place, which means it won't be strewn throughout your home.

The Daily Purge

My kids do two things each day that helps reduce clutter, garbage accumulation, and the tendency for lost articles of clothing, equipment, or schoolbooks: After we return home at the end of each day, they empty the car of all their belongings and any garbage that has accumulated. Next, as soon as they walk in the door from school or other activities, they go through their backpacks. They then give me important handouts or papers from school, locate their homework or other assignments, and throw away any garbage!

21. Teach Kids to Clean Up After Themselves

Kids will never learn to take care of their stuff, clean their rooms, make their beds, or put away their clothes if you do it for them. You need to make them do it. How? Refuse to do it yourself. And keep telling them that it's their responsibility. After they have either forgotten an assignment or lost their wallets and have no access to their money, they will start to keep a tidier room. If a bedroom becomes too unruly, I will come in and dump out their drawers. I'll bring a trash can and say, "It's clean-out time!" But remember this: Kids don't have long-term memories, so don't expect them to remember to clean up after themselves without your repeating the message many times! Don't hesitate to remind them again and again to clean up after themselves, and don't be afraid to use consequences if necessary!

Healthy Habits That Last a Lifetime

22. Select the Right Pediatrician for You

Finding a pediatrician is like getting married—it's a long-term relationship and breaking up is stressful. So you want to do your homework. Make sure you select a pediatrician who shares your philosophy and style regarding handling children's health issues, both mental and physical. Once you select a pediatrician, it's important to develop a relationship with him or her.

I have used the same pediatrician for all my children. He is very laid-back and relates well to the kids from the youngest to my teenagers. When the kids reach adolescence, he talks to them privately—without me—for a frank discussion about how their bodies are changing. He does not give the shots. Instead he lets the nurses do this—a great idea that prevents the kids from associating him with fear and unpleasantness. I love our doctor, and my kids sense this and love him too.

How to find the right doctor?

I have found that word of mouth is best, so don't be shy about quizzing your friends. Is the doctor laid-back or alarmist? When you call, can you get through quickly? What about his bedside manner? Is he or she quick to prescribe medications or is he willing to seek alternatives? Discussing these topics with others who've had direct experience really helps in developing an opinion about a good match.

Make sure your kids like your pediatrician. You don't have to overthink this. You can easily observe younger kids' responses to doctors, and older kids will share the information with you.

But most important, trust your instincts. Ask yourself: As you establish a relationship with your children's doctor, do you understand the issues well? If you don't, is this your problem or is the doctor not explaining things clearly? Is he or she condescending or respectful of your need to know? Will it bother you if the doctor sends you to the ER for a high fever, or do you want to play it safe in every case? Sometimes you won't know what kind of parent you are in regard to these kinds of issues until you are faced with them. When you figure it out, finding the right pediatrician will calm your nerves.

Should you find yourself in a medical emergency, feeling in sync—at that daunting moment—with the one person who is your right arm will help you tackle obstacles with confidence in God's divine plan.

23. Create Bedtime Routines

Sleep is crucial for kids' physical, mental, and emotional well-being. And while there are a ton of ways (and books to prove it!) to help kids sleep on their own, go back to sleep, and sleep in their own beds, one simple rule that's often overlooked is the importance of maintaining a consistent bedtime routine.

It is easier to construct bedtime rituals when the kids are young. We use a bedtime ritual that consists of take a bath, say prayers, tell stories, and turn out the light. I never sat in the room with a child and rocked him or her to sleep. I knew the kids were tired, so I put them in bed and without much fanfare said, "See ya tomorrow." This has always worked for me.

Of course there have been plenty of instances in which children had trouble settling down after a particularly busy day or woke up in the middle of the night after a nightmare and had trouble falling back to sleep. In such cases, I've

- taught the kids to say the Rosary, which is very soothing. If you're not religious, you can have them memorize a poem or nursery rhyme.
- laid down next to them and either read them a story or simply rubbed their backs.
- and sometimes I've taken them into my bed to sleep between Jim and me.

As kids get older, they have so much to do before going to bed—homework, being the main thing. Now the older kids are dying to go to sleep but can't until they finish everything.

Bedtime routines are important because they help calm kids down at the end of long, busy days. If they are not calm, then they will not rest or sleep as well. And we all know what overtired kids are like!

Shiny Teeth Make the Brightest Smiles

Brush, brush, brush your teeth! Kids need to brush their teeth after each meal and they need to understand the consequences of not brushing. Do they know they can develop cavities? Gingivitis? Gum disease? Bad breath? Don't be afraid to be descriptive so that your kids connect cause and effect when it comes to brushing their teeth and flossing!

You also need to remember to set yearly or bi-annual checkups with the dentist. Make sure the dentist is friendly and gets along with kids. There is a reason children become fearful of going to the dentist: Sometimes dentists are less than tender when explaining what they are going to do, and then what they do hurts. So it's best to prepare your kids for the dentist. The next time you or an older child has a dentist appointment, take your young child along with you. Let the him or her sit in the dentist's chair, swivel around, and become comfortable. That way, when the time comes for his or her initial visit, the place—and the dentist—will be more familiar.

24. Make Exercise a Regular Part of Your Kids' Day

We all know how important it is that our kids get enough physical exercise and activity. It's crucial to their physical health, their emotional well-being, and proper growth and maturation. And while some kids are naturally interested in sports—or just running around outside—and find ways to get exercise without even thinking, other kids tend to need a bit of a push or touch of encouragement to find a form of exercise they enjoy and will do on a regular basis.

When I was a kid, my parents simply said, "Go outside and play," and that's exactly what my sisters and I did. Today, all my kids are active. They play sports after school and on weekends. And when they are home, they run around our backyard, ride bikes up and down the driveway, and never stop moving. We're lucky that our kids have taken to sports so easily. We don't have to worry about them getting enough exercise. But even the least athletically inclined kids can find some sort of exercise or sport-related activity they will like so they can benefit.

If you have trouble (or if your kids are giving you trouble) getting involved in physical activity, consider these tips:

• Expose your kids to various sports by taking them to see practice sessions or games by other kids or professionals.
• Let them make the choice. Kids are more likely to try a new activity or sport if it's one that appeals to them.

- Research local teams and clubs. Not all of them are right for all kids. Some teams are hard-core, which means they're more competitive than others. A less competitive team is better suited for a child trying a sport for the first time.
- Establish a relationship with the coach or instructor, but don't get overinvolved. Simply give the coach information about your child's personality, temperament, or other specifics that might be helpful.

Here are some not-so-common sports to look into:

Karate—This is both an art and a sport and engages both the mind and the body as children learn intricate rules and the ability to concentrate for long periods of time.

Swimming—Kids can benefit from swimming without getting involved in competition. Sign your children up for swim classes or a free swim program to get them moving!

Horseback Riding—Although it can be expensive, kids who love animals are completely wowed by this wonderful, engaging activity.

Dance—Some kids love to move to the music. Many towns offer tap, ballet, or jazz classes at all levels, for all ages.

Camping—If your child likes the outdoors, then get him or her involved in camping. Although organizations like Boy Scouts and Girl Scouts offer camping trips, there are other ways children can acquire camping skills, grow confidence in their physical stamina, and learn to get along in the outdoors.

Table Tennis—This sport is the most popular sport in Asia and the second most popular sport in Europe (after soccer), and it recently became an Olympic sport. Tennis table clubs are popping up in many areas, so look for one near your community. You can even hold family tournaments!

Bowling—Bowling is not just for older men and ladies! Kids love to bowl! Check out kids' programs in your area.

Build a tree house!

Childhood Obesity Is an Epidemic

National statistics show that close to one-third of all children living in the United States today are obese. This startling—but not new—figure points to a need for new thinking. Here are some important ways that you can help your children maintain a healthy weight:

Limit fast food. We all resort to it once in a while. It's quick, easy, and cheap. But fast food is highly processed with lots of added fat, salt, and other unhealthy ingredients.

Don't buy or stock a lot of sugary snacks or fatty junk food. When kids are hungry, they go hunting in your refrigerator or cupboard. If the junk food is there, they will eat it. If fruits or veggies are easily available, they will be more likely to have a healthy snack.

Teach your kids about nutrition. (See next page.) The more kids know about the food they eat, the more they will think about what food to eat.

Teach Your Kids About Food

Don't be afraid to teach your kids about the contents and purposes of the foods they eat. The more they understand what foods are made of and why their bodies need different nutrients—carbohydrates, proteins, fat, fiber, and sugar—they'll be in a better position to make healthy food choices. Kids as young as four can begin to understand what certain foods do for their bodies.

Here's a quick breakdown of how food is used by kids' bodies:

Carbs are necessary to fuel and maintain energy, both physical and mental.

Proteins are necessary to build and grow strong muscle tissues.

Fiber is necessary for proper digestion, the processing of carbohydrates, and the reduction of fat and cholesterol in the blood.

Fats are necessary for proper brain functioning and the health of the skin.

Sugar and starch, in moderation, help maintain blood sugar levels. Too much can lead to blood sugar disorders such as type 2 diabetes.

25. Set Up a Healthy Food Attitude

Kids learn food habits from you. You can offer them all the healthy, nutritious food in the world, but you have to practice what you preach if you want them to eat right today—and years down the road when you're no longer feeding them.

I always offer a balanced meal that contains a meat or fish, at least one vegetable or salad, and a carbohydrate. I generally keep a big bowl of cut fruit out on the counter so the kids can pick at it throughout the day. If it's in sight, they are more likely to go for it! I fill the bowl with strawberries, blueberries, raspberries, bananas, oranges, and pineapple. I try to cook as often as possible and avoid drive-thrus, but we are on the road a lot and sometimes we do stop and pick up fast food. But I usually don't let them have dark soda and light only occasionally. Normally they drink milk or water with meals.

Our kids learn habits from us. I am not overly strict about food, and I sometimes let them eat potato chips for breakfast, eat sweets, and the occasional fast food. But, I know that if I model good eating habits, they will follow in my footsteps with encouragement and reminders.

Diets Can Be Dangerous

It's good to encourage discussions about eating habits. Though the only kids who partake in special diets in our house are some of my boys who want to gain weight for football, there are plenty of kids and teens out there who begin to diet without their parents realizing it. Diets can be dangerous, especially if kids are dieting to look good or to follow their peers. It's the mentality behind the dieting that leads to the most serious problems. If kids begin to binge, purge, or think about food as their enemy, then they have developed a negative relationship with food. Parents (especially mothers who are watching their weight) can add to the problem by either commenting on a child who may have gained a few pounds or by continually harping on a child's eating habits.

When kids understand what their bodies need for good nutrition, they're more likely to eat what they like in moderation, and learn to make good choices that help their bodies feel good. They will eat wisely and well. If you suspect that one of your kids may have begun to skip meals or has trouble knowing when to stop, it's time to talk about what's going on. If a problem persists, don't hesitate to seek the advice of a professional with expertise on eating issues.

School and the Walls Beyond the Home

26. Limit Exposure to Violence

As much as we would like to, we cannot shelter our children from learning about or being hurt by the real world. When our children are young and don't understand the significance of a tsunami in Asia or a war in Iraq, it's easy to keep the facts and events of the world beyond the safety of our homes. But as they get older—indeed as soon as they go to school, learn to read, and visit friends' homes—we can no longer act as constant gatekeepers of information.

Our kids will be exposed to violence, death, heartache, and other types of negative news, and for that reason, we must prepare them by teaching them how to react to or manage such information. We can start by limiting exposure to violence. With that in mind, I rarely let my small children watch the news, play violent video games, or watch inappropriate movies. The studies are clear: When kids are exposed to violence, they are more apt to be violent—either in practice or in their minds. For this reason, I restrict television watching to kid-friendly shows and sports until children are 15 years old.

Exposure to this level of violence causes children to

"normalize" violence and become insensitive to the outcome of such acts. As parents we need to instill in our children from a very young age that hurting others in any way is wrong. Jim and I always pair this message by telling our kids that prayer and faith in God are necessary to create peace in the world and make it a better place.

When kids are old enough to understand the context of world events, they are better able to keep the significance of events in perspective. As they grow, they will learn how to handle information—whether painful, violent, or frightening—so that it doesn't get mixed in with false conclusions or inaccurate assumptions.

27. Know Your Child's School

Walking the fine line between being an involved parent and a pushy one can be tricky. How can we be interested without being nosy? The truth of the matter is that children of parents who are in the know about their children's academic environment get much more out of school. It's better for everyone involved: the kids, the teachers, and the parents.

Of course there is a difference between keeping your eyes open and asking good questions and being intrusive or second-guessing. The idea is to reach a comfort level where communication is easy and frequent and no questions or problems fester.

Do you know your children's principal? Their teachers? Are you aware of additions or cuts in extracurricular or core activities? While teachers don't like to feel scrutinized, they do like to know that parents care about what and how they're teaching. I think it's important to learn about the different classes and teachers and the experiences of other parents. This helps me put my particular child's concerns into better perspective.

One week after the first day of school, my then six-year-old came up to the car where I was in carpool line, saying that his new teacher would not call him by the family nickname. While still in line, I picked up my cell phone, dialed the school, and asked to speak with our son's teacher. I introduced myself and told her what a pleasure it was for my son to have such a fine teacher. I also made sure she knew that he was already enjoying her class. I then explained how everyone in our lives referred to our son by his nickname and my husband and I would appreciate her using this loving name as well. She got the message, and I didn't have to make the moment into a complaint.

It's easier to deal with such situations when you make it a point to get comfortable in the classroom. Perhaps you can volunteer during library time, serve lunch at school, or volunteer to drive kids on class field trips. Of course it's very important to attend parent/teacher conferences so you can communicate directly with your child's teacher about his or her academic performance, conduct, and general development and growth. Although it's always parents who know their children best, teachers often shed light on how children are becoming socialized. Do they get along with

School Rules

Post the school calendar.

Read all school notices sent home.

Attend teacher conferences.

Visit your child's classroom.

Don't do your child's homework.

their peers? Is it easy or difficult for them to make friends, join a group, or ask someone to play or participate in a partner activity? A teacher's perspective can help fill in the blanks if your child doesn't always come to you or describe a situation fully. The more you know about your child's classroom experience, the better help you can be to him or her outside of school—and inside school.

It's important that parents explain the school's rules or expectations to their kids. You may remember that I am a

Homework Is Kids' Work

There is no excuse for either doing your children's homework or letting them not do it. I recommend that kids do their homework immediately after school rather than putting it off until the evening when they are tired and more distracted. When the kids are doing their homework, I try to make the experience as fun and comfortable as possible by offering snacks and simply being present to let them know I care. I want them to associate homework with good feelings. Mom or Dad's presence means a lot to kids, especially if they encounter difficulty or frustration. Indeed, if you notice that a child needs extra help to understand a concept or learn how to study in a different way and you don't feel comfortable, then you may need to arrange for a tutor. My point is this: Kids don't need you to do their homework; but they do need to know that you care about their homework getting done.

former teacher, and I saw the damage done by so-called "rescue moms" who always solve their kids' problems for them. If your child forgets her homework, it may not always be a good idea to race down to school. If you don't, maybe she'll remember to bring it the next time. School is a place for learning—first and foremost—and parents need to foster their kids' abilities to learn, not do it for them.

Developing a longer-term view on school issues also helps keep things in perspective. I like to know about the teacher turnover rate and where kids go after matriculating. This gives me a sense of the overall atmosphere of the school and the direction it is heading academically. Not every school is the right one for every child, and I might as well be in the know from the get-go.

But most important is to remember that you are your child's advocate, and this means standing up for your child, informing his or her teacher of any emotional or physical issues your child may be dealing with, and communicating any major changes that have occurred at home or in the child's life so the teacher understands the context of your child's behavior.

28. Oversee Their Organized Sports

Organized sports in this country have become way too serious. Practice on Sundays. Practice until 8 p.m. on a school night. Club teams and school teams. They are highly demanding and require both parents and kids to make an enormous commitment of time, energy, and money. My children could and would like to play everything, but for all the above reasons, Jim and I have decided to restrict our kids to playing one sport per season. (We also restrict them from playing on more than one team. For example, we allow our kids to play on either the school soccer team or a select "club" team.) We also don't allow them to play sports on Sundays—even if a coach says our child will be barred from playing.

It's important to encourage kids to try various sports or find a new sport they might be better suited for. For instance, when one of my boys found wrestling, he introduced the entire family to a new sport. The other kids were impressed and cheered him on.

Sports are great for building confidence and growing positive self-esteem. However, they need to remain a source of enjoyment, not discomfort or pressure. Parents should keep this in mind as they head to the stands to cheer their kids on!

29. Sex, Drugs, and Rock 'n' Roll

In this day and age, parents cannot avoid the reality that sex, drugs, and rock 'n' roll are out there, ready to influence our kids. I have established a very open line of communication with my kids on these topics. I want them to feel comfortable enough to talk to me. I let them know that I know what's going on. Sometimes it's clear that they think that if a certain incident or situation is not discussed, it's like it never happens. But I know it does happen. I'm talking here about drinking alcohol at parties, sexual encounters, and doing drugs.

For Jim and me, it's all about helping prepare our kids for the reality of what's out there, giving them accurate reliable information about what happens when kids drink, take drugs, and have sex, and making them feel confident enough to resist the pressure to participate. We give the birds and bees talk when kids reach age twelve, checking in with them all the time. We continue to remind them that drugs are bad for the body and brain, that they're a detriment to school and sports.

We can't always be by our kids' sides to help them negotiate these troubling obstacles, but we can do our best to talk to them about what is right and wrong, healthy and nonhealthy, and moral and immoral. We can give them support, encouragement, and lead by example. And we can pray.

30. Keep Talking

Kids rarely talk about certain subjects without being prompted. When you take the initiative, you keep the door open for back-and-forth communication. It's this open and caring communication that helps build their trust in you because they know you know and understand what's going on in their lives. In turn, they will feel closer to you and will be more likely to come to you for more serious problems.

The Top Six Funniest Things My Kids Have Said or Done

As the mother of ten, I've had quite a bit come from the mouths of babes. Here are some of the most interesting:

1. When one of our sons was a little guy and learning how to take care of himself after going to the bathroom, he was having a hard time wiping and said, "Why didn't Jesus put my butt in the front instead of the back where I could see it?"

2. When one of our sons was just a little guy playing baseball and not connecting very well with the ball, we told him to choke up on the bat. He started coughing and making choking sounds toward the bat!

3. One time one of our sons was playing T-ball and was getting very bored. In the middle of the game he just walked off the field and told us he wanted a bagel with cream cheese.

They'll trust you and your open door policy.

I often do my best talking in the car—(can't understand why since I spend an average of just about eight hours a day in my car!). Jim and I make it a point to always be approachable so our kids will talk to us and will come to us for advice and help in solving their problems. Though sometimes we feel exhausted or are in the middle of some activity or conversation, we always try to go back to that child and say, "What's up? You wanted to talk to me?"

4. Another son was starting a new preschool called Carmelite Child Development. The teachers are mainly Carmelite sisters in full habit. After the first day of school, our son came home and asked me, "Why are all my teachers from *Sister Act 2*?"

5. Our son flushed some clothes down the toilet one day. We scolded him, saying, "Don't flush your clothes down the toilet." He responded, "They're not my clothes; they're Big's." (Big is his little brother.)

6. Every time we go to this one shopping mall, we can never find a parking place. So one time when we arrived at the parking lot, I asked everyone in the car to start praying to the Blessed Mother to help us find a parking spot. All of a sudden, right near us, a car began backing out, and I said, "See, I told you—look!" The kids started shouting, "Where is she?" and began frantically looking out the window, thinking that the Blessed Mother was driving!

Parents need to listen without being immediately critical so kids learn to trust them. This is especially true for parents of teenagers—the time when kids tend to put distance between them and their parents.

It's difficult to hear some of our children's situations and feelings. We worry, we become afraid for them, we want to protect them. One time one of my sons told me he saw an inappropriate pop-up on the computer. Normally I keep the parental controls on, but sometimes a power failure switches them off. I was dismayed by the pornographic content of the pop-ups, but I was glad that my son told me about them. It meant two things: that he was living by the values we have been teaching him and that he trusts me.

It is of utmost importance that you honor the confidentiality of these serious discussions. When kids trust their parents, they are more likely to confide in them about dangerous or potentially dangerous circumstances. You don't want to be the last person to know, and you certainly want to know before it's too late.

Acknowledgments

Writing this book has been a labor of love, for which I have many people to thank for their inspiration, encouragement, and support.

I first would like to thank my family, from whom I have received so very much. My own parents have loved me unconditionally and have been a constant support to me throughout my life. I am so grateful for my mom's youthful, open-hearted, and selfless spirit. I am equally thankful to my dad for being such a man's man, but to me the most gentle, loving man and father, always full of love and full of life. I also wish to thank my parents-in-law who have raised eight children of their own and have been role models to me of how to successfully raise a wonderful family. My mother-in-law's constant spiritual guidance and charitable consciousness and my father-in-law's wisdom and leadership have truly been an inspiration. I wish to also thank my sisters, my sisters-in-law, and my brothers-in-law who have been tireless in their support and encouragement—to them I extend big hugs all around. I also wish to acknowledge the spirit of my children's Greek-Italian-Lebanese heritage. The wisdom passed down from the generations continues to inspire and drive me in all I do.

I would like to thank my wonderful agents, Kim Witherspoon, Richard Pine, and David Forrer, for their belief in me and never-ending support and guidance. I would also like to thank Billie Fitzpatrick, my collaborator, who helped me shape my thoughts and feelings into words on the page. The Meredith team, including Linda Cunningham and Denise Caringer, have been absolutely wonderful to work with, and I am so grateful that my book landed in their corner.

Finally I want to extend a special thank you to all my dear friends (who are also women, wives, and mothers), especially Cathy Graham, whose enthusiasm, advice, and constant support during the course of writing this book have been so valuable.